Convent Affairs

Jacques Casanova de Seingalt

[ZHINGOORA BOOKS]

CONVENT AFFAIRS

CHAPTER XVI

Countess Coronini—A Lover's Pique—Reconciliation—The First Meeting—A
Philosophical Parenthesis

My beautiful nun had not spoken to me, and I was glad of it, for I was so astonished, so completely under the spell of her beauty, that I might have given her a very poor opinion of my intelligence by the rambling answers which I should very likely have given to her questions. I knew her to be certain that she had not to fear the humiliation of a refusal from me, but I admired her courage in running the risk of it in her position. I could hardly understand her boldness, and I could not conceive how she contrived to enjoy so much liberty. A casino at Muran! the possibility of going to Venice to sup with a young man! It was all very surprising, and I decided in my own mind that she had an acknowledged lover whose pleasure it was to make her happy by satisfying her caprices. It is true that such a thought was rather unpleasant to my pride, but there was too much piquancy in the adventure, the heroine of it was too attractive, for me to be stopped by any considerations. I saw very well that I was taking the high road to become unfaithful to my dear C—— C——, or rather that I was already so in thought and will, but I must confess that, in spite of all my love for that charming child, I felt no qualms of conscience. It seemed to me that an infidelity of that sort, if she ever heard of it, would not displease her, for that short excursion on strange ground would only keep me alive and in good condition for her, because it would save me from the weariness which was surely killing me.

I had been presented to the celebrated Countess Coronini by a nun, a relative of M. Dandolo. That countess, who had been very handsome and was very witty, having made up her mind to renounce the political intrigues which had been the study of her whole life, had sought a retreat in the Convent of St. Justine, in the hope of finding in that refuge the calm which she wanted, and which her disgust of society had rendered necessary to her. As she had enjoyed a very great reputation, she was still visited at the convent by all the foreign ambassadors and by the first noblemen of Venice; inside of the walls of her convent the countess was acquainted with everything that happened in the city. She always received me very kindly, and, treating me as a young man, she took pleasure in giving me, every time I called on her, very agreeable lessons in morals. Being quite certain to find out from her, with a little manoeuvering, something concerning M——M——, I decided on paying her a visit the day after I had seen the beautiful nun.

The countess gave me her usual welcome, and, after the thousand nothings which it is the custom to utter in society before anything worth saying is spoken, I led the conversation up to the convents of Venice. We spoke of the wit and influence of a nun called Celsi, who, although ugly, had an immense credit everywhere and in everything. We mentioned afterwards the young and lovely Sister Michali, who had taken the veil to prove to her mother that she was superior to her in intelligence and wit. After speaking of several other nuns who had the reputation of being addicted to gallantry, I named M—— M——, remarking that most likely she deserved that reputation likewise, but that she was an enigma. The countess answered with a smile that she was not an enigma for everybody, although she was necessarily so for most people.

"What is incomprehensible," she said, "is the caprice that she took suddenly to become a nun, being handsome, rich, free, well-educated, full of wit, and, to my knowledge, a Free-thinker. She took the veil without any reason, physical or moral; it was a mere caprice."

"Do you believe her to be happy, madam?"

"Yes, unless she has repented her decision, or if she does not repent it some day. But if ever she does, I think she will be wise enough never to say so to anyone."

Satisfied by the mysterious air of the countess that M—— M—— had a lover, I made up my mind not to trouble myself about it, and having put on my mask I went to Muran in the afternoon. When I reached the gate of the convent I rang the bell, and with an anxious heart I asked for M—— M—— in the name of Madame de S——. The small parlour being closed, the attendant pointed out to me the one in which I had to go. I went in, took off my mask, and sat down waiting for my divinity.

My heart was beating furiously; I was waiting with great impatience; yet that expectation was not without charm, for I dreaded the beginning of the interview. An hour passed pretty rapidly, but I began then to find the time rather long, and thinking that, perhaps, the attendant had not rightly understood me, I rang the bell, and enquired whether notice of my visit had being given to Sister M—— M——. A voice answered affirmatively. I took my seat again, and a few minutes afterwards an old, toothless nun came in and informed me that Sister M—— M—— was engaged for the whole day. Without giving me time to utter a single word, the woman left the parlour. This was one of those terrible moments to which the man who worships at the shrine of the god of love is exposed! They are indeed cruel moments; they bring fearful sorrow, they may cause death.

Feeling myself disgraced, my first sensation was utter contempt for myself, an inward despair which was akin to rage; the second was disdainful indignation against the nun, upon whom I passed the severe judgment which I thought she deserved, and which was the only way I had to soothe my grief. Such behaviour proclaimed her to be the most impudent of women, and entirely wanting in good sense; for the two letters she had written to me were quite enough to ruin her character if I had wished to revenge myself, and she evidently could not expect anything else from me. She must have been mad to set at defiance my revengeful feelings, and I should certainly have thought that she was insane if I had not heard her converse with the countess.

Time, they say, brings good counsel; it certainly brings calm, and cool reflection gives lucidity to the mind. At last I persuaded myself that what had occurred was after all in no way extraordinary, and that I would certainly have considered it at first a very common occurrence if I had not been dazzled by the wonderful beauty of the nun, and blinded by my own vanity. As a very natural result I felt that I was at liberty to laugh at my mishap, and that nobody could possibly guess whether my mirth was genuine or only counterfeit. Sophism is so officious!

But, in spite of all my fine arguments, I still cherished the thought of revenge; no debasing element, however, was to form part of it, and being determined not to leave the person who had been guilty of such a bad practical joke the slightest cause of triumph, I had the courage not to shew any vexation. She had sent word to me that she was engaged; nothing more natural; the part I had to play was to appear indifferent. "Most likely she will not be engaged another time," I said to myself, "but I defy her to catch me in the snare again. I mean to shew her that I only laugh at her uncivil behaviour." Of course I intended to send back her letters, but not without the accompaniment of a billet-doux, the gallantry of which was not likely to please her.

The worse part of the affair for me was to be compelled to go to her church; because, supposing her not to be aware of my going there for C—— C——, she might imagine that the only object of my visits was to give her the opportunity of apologizing for her conduct and of appointing a new meeting. I wanted her to entertain no doubt of my utter contempt for her person, and I felt certain that she had proposed the other meetings in Venice and at the casino of Muran only to deceive me more easily.

I went to bed with a great thirst for revenge, I fell asleep thinking of it, and I awoke with the resolution of quenching it. I began to write, but, as I wished particularly that my letter should not show the pique of the disappointed lover, I left it on my table with the intention of reading it again the next day. It proved a useful precaution, for when I read it over, twenty-four hours afterwards, I found it unworthy of me, and tore it to pieces. It contained some sentences which savoured too much of my weakness, my love, and my spite, and which, far from humiliating her, would only have given her occasion to laugh at me.

On the Wednesday after I had written to C—— C—— that very serious reasons compelled me to give up my visits to the church of her convent, I wrote another letter to the nun, but on Thursday it had the same fate as the first, because upon a second perusal I found the same deficiencies. It seemed to me that I had lost the faculty of writing. Ten days afterwards I found out that I was too deeply in love to have the power of expressing myself in any other way than through the feelings of my heart.

'Sincerium est nisi vas, quodcunque infundis acescit.'

The face of M—— M—— had made too deep an impression on me; nothing could possibly obliterate it except the all-powerful influence of time.

In my ridiculous position I was sorely tempted to complain to Countess S——; but I am happy to say I was prudent enough not to cross the threshold of her door. At last I bethought myself that the giddy nun was certainly labouring under constant dread, knowing that I had in my possession her two letters, with which I could ruin her reputation and cause the greatest injury to the convent, and I sent them back to her with the following note, after I had kept them ten days:

"I can assure you, madam, that it was owing only to forgetfulness that I did not return your two letters which you will find enclosed. I have never thought of belying my own nature by taking a cowardly revenge upon you, and I forgive you most willingly the two giddy acts of which you have been guilty, whether they were committed thoughtlessly or because you wanted to enjoy a joke at my expense. Nevertheless, you will allow me to advise you not to treat any other man in the same way, for you might meet with one endowed with less delicacy. I know your name, I know who you are, but you need not be anxious; it is exactly as if I did not know it. You may, perhaps, care but little for my discretion, but if it should be so I should greatly pity you.

"You may be aware that I shall not shew myself again at your church; but let me assure you that it is not a sacrifice on my part, and that I can attend mass anywhere else. Yet I must tell you why I shall abstain from frequenting the church of your convent. It is very natural for me to suppose that to the two thoughtless acts of which you have been guilty, you have added another not less serious, namely, that of having boasted of your exploits with the other nuns, and I do not want to be the butt of your jokes in cell or parlour. Do not think me too ridiculous if, in spite of being five or six years older than you, I have not thrown off all feelings of self-respect, or trodden under, my feet all reserve and propriety; in one word, if I have kept some prejudices, there are a few which in my opinion ought never to be forgotten. Do not disdain, madam, the lesson which I take the liberty to teach you, as I receive in the kindest spirit the one which you have given me, most likely only for the sake of fun, but by which I promise you to profit as long as I live."

I thought that, considering all circumstances, my letter was a very genial one; I made up my parcel, put on my mask, and looked out for a porter who could have no knowledge of me; I gave him half a sequin, and I promised him as much more when he could assure me that he had faithfully delivered my letter at the convent of Muran. I gave him all the necessary instructions, and cautioned him to go away the very moment he had delivered the letter at the gate of the convent, even if he were told to wait. I must say here that my messenger was a man from Forli, and that the Forlanese were then the most trustworthy men in Venice; for one of them to be guilty of a breach of trust was an unheard-of thing. Such men were formerly the Savoyards, in Paris; but everything is getting worse in this world.

I was beginning to forget the adventure, probably because I thought, rightly or wrongly, that I had put an insurmountable barrier between the nun and myself, when, ten days after I had sent my letter, as I was coming out of the opera, I met my messenger, lantern in hand. I called him, and without taking off my mask I asked him whether he knew me. He looked at me, eyed me from head to foot, and finally answered that he did not.

"Did you faithfully carry the message to Muran?"

"Ah, sir! God be praised! I am very happy to see you again, for I have an important communication to make to you. I took your letter, delivered it according to your instructions, and I went away as soon as it was in the hands of the attendant, although she requested me to wait. When I returned from Muran I did not see you, but that did not matter. On the following day, one of my companions, who happened to be at the gate of the convent when I delivered your letter, came early in the morning to tell me to go to Muran, because the attendant wanted particularly to speak to me. I went there, and after waiting for a few minutes I was shewn into the parlour, where I was kept for more than an hour by a nun as beautiful as the light of day, who asked me a thousand questions for the purpose of ascertaining, if not who you are, at least where I should be likely to find you. You know that I could not give her any satisfactory information. She then left the parlour, ordering me to wait, and at the end of two hours she came back with a letter which she entrusted to my hands, telling me that, if I succeeded in finding you out and in bringing her an answer, she would give me two sequins. In the mean time I was to call at the convent every day, shew her the letter, and receive forty sons every time. Until now I have earned twenty crowns, but I am afraid the lady will get tired of it, and you can make me earn two sequins by answering a line."

"Where is the letter?"

"In my room under lock and key, for I am always afraid of losing it."

"Then how can I answer?"

"If you will wait for me here, you shall have the letter in less than a quarter of an hour."

"I will not wait, because I do not care about the letter. But tell me. how you could flatter the nun with the hope of finding me out? You are a rogue, for it is not likely that she would have trusted you with the letter if you had not promised her to find me."

"I am not a rogue, for I have done faithfully what you told me; but it is true that I gave her a description of your coat, your buckles, and your figure, and I can assure you that for the last ten days I have examined all the masks who are about your size, but in vain. Now I recognize your buckles, but I do not think you have the same coat. Alas, sir! it will not cost you much to write only one line. Be kind enough to wait for me in the coffee-house close by."

I could not resist my curiosity any longer, and I made up my mind not to wait for him but to accompany him as far as his house. I had only to write, "I have received the letter," and my curiosity was gratified and the Forlanese earned his two sequins. I could afterwards change my buckles and my mask, and thus set all enquiries at defiance.

I therefore followed him to his door; he went in and brought me the letter. I took him to an inn, where I asked for a room with a good fire, and I told my man to wait. I broke the seal of the parcel—a rather large one, and the first papers that I saw were the two letters which I had sent back to her in order to allay her anxiety as to the possible consequences of her giddiness.

The sight of these letters caused me such a palpitation of the heart that
I was compelled to sit down: it was a most evident sign of my

defeat.

Besides these two letters I found a third one signed "S." and addressed

to M—— M——. I read the following lines:

"The mask who accompanied me back to my house would not, I believe, have uttered a single word, if I had not told him that the charms of your witty mind were even more bewitching than those of your person; and his answer was, 'I have seen the one, and I believe in the other.' I added that I did not understand why you had not spoken to him, and he said, with a smile, 'I refused to be presented to her, and she punished me for it by not appearing to know that I was present.' These few words were all our dialogue. I intended to send you this note this morning, but found it impossible. Adieu."

After reading this note, which stated the exact truth, and which could be considered as proof, my heart began to beat less quickly. Delighted at seeing myself on the point of being convicted of injustice, I took courage, and I read the following letter:

"Owing to an excusable weakness, feeling curious to know what you would say about me to the countess after you had seen me, I took an opportunity of asking her to let me know all you said to her on the following day at latest, for I foresaw that you would pay me a visit in the afternoon. Her letter, which I enclose, and which I beg you to read, did not reach me till half an hour after you had left the convent.

"This was the first fatality.

"Not having received that letter when you called, I had not the courage to see you. This absurd weakness on my part was the second fatality, but the weakness you will; I hope; forgive. I gave orders to the lay-sister to tell you that I was ill for the whole day; a very legitimate excuse; whether true or false, for it was an officious untruth, the correction of which, was to be found in the words: for the whole day. You had already left the convent, and I could not possibly send anyone to run after you, when the old fool informed me of her having told you that I was engaged.

"This was the third fatality.

"You cannot imagine what I had a mind to do and to say to that foolish sister; but here one must say or do nothing; one must be patient and dissemble, thanking God when mistakes are the result of ignorance and not of wickedness—a very common thing in convents. I foresaw at once, at least partly; what would happen; and what has actually, happened; for no reasonable being could, I believe, have foreseen it all. I guessed that, thinking yourself the victim of a joke, you would be incensed, and I felt miserable, for I did not see any way of letting you know the truth before the following Sunday. My heart longed ardently for that day. Could I possibly imagine that you, would take a resolution not to come again to our church! I tried to be patient until that Sunday; but when I found myself disappointed in my hope, my misery became unbearable, and it will cause my death if you refuse to listen to my justification. Your letter has made me completely unhappy, and I shall not resist my despair if you persist in the cruel resolve expressed by your unfeeling letter. You have considered yourself trifled with; that is all you can say; but will this letter convince you of your error? And even believing yourself deceived in the most scandalous manner, you must admit that to write such an awful letter you must have supposed me an abominable wretch—a monster, such as a woman of noble birth and of refined education cannot possibly be. I enclose the two letters you sent back to me, with the idea of allaying my fears which you cruelly supposed very different to what they are in reality. I am a better physiognomist than you, and you must be quite certain that I have not acted thoughtlessly, for I never thought you capable, I will not say of crime, but even of an indelicate action. You must have read on my features the signs only of giddy impudence, and that is not my nature. You may be the cause of my death, you will certainly make me miserable for the remainder of my life, if you do not justify yourself; on my side I think the justification is complete.

"I hope that, even if you feel no interest in my life, you will think that you are bound in honour to come and speak to me. Come yourself to recall all you have written; it is your duty, and I deserve it. If you do not realize the fatal effect produced upon me by your letter, I must indeed pity you, in spite of my misery, for it proves that you have not the slightest knowledge of the human heart. But I feel certain that you will come back, provided the man to whom I trust this letter contrives to find you. Adieu! I expect life or death from you."

I did not require to read that letter twice; I was ashamed and in despair. M—— M—— was right. I called the Forlanese, enquired from him whether he had spoken to her in the morning, and whether she looked ill. He answered that he had found her looking

15

more unhappy every day, and that her eyes were red from weeping.

"Go down again and wait," I said to him.

I began to write, and I had not concluded my long screed before the dawn of day; here are, word by word, the contents of the letter which I wrote to the noblest of women, whom in my unreasonable spite I had judged so wrongly.

"I plead guilty, madam; I cannot possibly justify myself, and I am perfectly convinced of your innocence. I should be disconsolate if I did not hope to obtain pardon, and you will not refuse to forgive me if you are kind enough to recollect the cause of my guilt. I saw you; I was dazzled, and I could not realize a happiness which seemed to me a dream; I thought myself the prey of one of those delightful illusions which vanish when we wake up. The doubt under which I was labouring could not be cleared up for twenty-four hours, and how could I express my feverish impatience as I was longing for that happy moment! It came at last! and my heart, throbbing with desire and hope, was flying towards you while I was in the parlour counting the minutes! Yet an hour passed almost rapidly, and not unnaturally, considering my impatience and the deep impression I felt at the idea of seeing you. But then, precisely at the very moment when I believed myself certain that I was going to gaze upon the beloved features which had been in one interview indelibly engraved upon my heart, I saw the most disagreeable face appear, and a creature announced that you were engaged for the whole day, and without giving me time to utter one word she disappeared! You may imagine my astonishment and... the rest. The lightning would not have produced upon me a more rapid, a more terrible effect! If you had sent me a line by that sister—a line from your hand—I would have gone away, if not pleased, at least submissive and resigned.

"But that was a fourth fatality which you have forgotten to add to your delightful and witty justification. Thinking myself scoffed at, my self-love rebelled, and indignation for the moment silenced love. Shame overwhelmed me! I thought that everybody could read on my face all the horror in my heart, and I saw in you, under the outward appearance of an angel, nothing but a fearful daughter of the Prince of Darkness. My mind was thoroughly upset, and at the end of eleven days I lost the small portion of good sense that was left in me—at least I must suppose so, as it is then that I wrote to you the letter of which you have so good a right to complain, and which at that time seemed to me a masterpiece of moderation.

"But I hope it is all over now, and this very day at eleven o'clock you will see me at your feet—tender, submissive and repentant. You will forgive me, divine woman, or I will myself avenge you for the insult I have hurled at you. The only thing which I dare to ask from you as a great favour is to burn my first letter, and never to mention it again. I sent it only after I had written four, which I destroyed one after the other: you may therefore imagine the state of my heart.

"I have given orders to my messenger to go to your convent at once, so that my letter can be delivered to you as soon as you wake in the morning. He would never have discovered me, if my good angel had not made me go up to him at the door of the opera-house. But I shall not require his services any more; do not answer me, and receive all the devotion of a heart which adores you."

When my letter was finished, I called my Forlanese, gave him one sequin, and I made him promise me to go to Muran immediately, and to deliver my letter only to the nun herself. As soon as he had gone I threw myself on my bed, but anxiety and burning impatience would not allow me to sleep.

I need not tell the reader who knows the state of excitement under which I was labouring, that I was punctual in presenting myself at the convent. I was shewn into the small parlour where I had seen her for the first time, and she almost immediately made her entrance. As soon as I saw her near the grating I fell on my knees, but she entreated me to rise at once as I might be seen. Her face was flushed with excitement, and her looks seemed to me heavenly. She sat down, and I took a seat opposite to her. We remained several minutes motionless, gazing at each other without speaking, but I broke the silence by asking her, in a voice full of love and anxiety, whether I could hope to obtain my pardon. She gave me her beautiful hand through the grating, and I covered it with tears and kisses.

"Our acquaintance," she said, "has begun with a violent storm; let us hope that we shall now enjoy it long in perfect and lasting calm. This is the first time that we speak to one another, but what has occurred must be enough to give us a thorough knowledge of each other. I trust that our intimacy will be as tender as sincere, and that we shall know how to have a mutual indulgence for our faults."

"Can such an angel as you have any?"

"Ah, my friend! who is without them?"

"When shall I have the happiness of convincing you of my devotion with complete freedom and in all the joy of my heart?"

"We will take supper together at my casino whenever you please, provided you give me notice two days beforehand; or I will go and sup with you in Venice, if it will not disturb your arrangements."

"It would only increase my happiness. I think it right to tell you that I am in very easy circumstances, and that, far from fearing expense, I delight in it: all I possess belongs to the woman I love."

"That confidence, my dear friend, is very agreeable to me, the more so that I have likewise to tell you that I am very rich, and that I could not refuse anything to my lover."

"But you must have a lover?"

"Yes; it is through him that I am rich, and he is entirely my master. I never conceal anything from him. The day after to-morrow, when I am alone with you, I will tell you more."

"But I hope that your lover...."

"Will not be there? Certainly not. Have you a mistress?"

"I had one, but, alas! she has been taken from me by violent means, and for the last six months I have led a life of complete celibacy."

"Do you love her still?"

"I cannot think of her without loving her. She has almost as great charms, as great beauty, as you have; but I foresee that you will make me forget her."

"If your happiness with her was complete, I pity you. She has been violently taken from you, and you shun society in order to feed your sorrow. I have guessed right, have I not? But if I happen to take possession of her place in your heart, no one, my sweet friend, shall turn me out of it."

"But what will your lover say?"

"He will be delighted to see me happy with such a lover as you. It is in his nature."

"What an admirable nature! Such heroism is quite beyond me!"

"What sort of a life do you lead in Venice?"

"I live at the theatres, in society, in the casinos, where I fight against fortune sometimes with good sometimes with bad success."

"Do you visit the foreign ambassadors?"

"No, because I am too much acquainted with the nobility; but I know them all."

"How can you know them if you do not see them?"

"I have known them abroad. In Parma the Duke de Montalegre, the Spanish ambassador; in Vienna I knew Count Rosemberg; in Paris, about two years ago, the French ambassador."

"It is near twelve o'clock, my dear friend; it is time for us to part. Come at the same hour the day after tomorrow, and I will give you all the instructions which you will require to enable you to come and sup with me."

"Alone?"

"Of course."

"May I venture to ask you for a pledge? The happiness which you promise me is so immense!"

"What pledge do you want?"

"To see you standing before that small window in the grating with permission for me to occupy the same place as Madame de S——."

She rose at once, and, with the most gracious smile, touched the spring; after a most expressive kiss, I took leave of her. She followed me with her eyes as far as the door, and her loving gaze would have rooted me to the spot if she had not left the room.

I spent the two days of expectation in a whirl of impatient joy, which prevented me from eating and sleeping; for it seemed to me that no other love had ever given me such happiness, or rather that I was going to be happy for the first time.

Irrespective of birth, beauty, and wit, which was the principal merit of my new conquest, prejudice was there to enhance a hundredfold my felicity, for she was a vestal: it was forbidden fruit, and who does not know that, from Eve down to our days, it was that fruit which has always appeared the most delicious! I was on the point of encroaching upon the rights of an all-powerful husband; in my eyes M—— M—— was above all the queens of the earth.

If my reason had not been the slave of passion, I should have known that my nun could not be a different creature from all the pretty women whom I had loved for the thirteen years that I had been labouring in the fields of love. But where is the man in love who can harbour such a thought? If it presents itself too often to his mind, he expels it disdainfully! M—— M—— could not by any means be otherwise than superior to all other women in the wide world.

Animal nature, which chemists call the animal kingdom, obtains through instinct the three various means necessary for the perpetuation of its species.

There are three real wants which nature has implanted in all human creatures. They must feed themselves, and to prevent that task from being insipid and tedious they have the agreeable sensation of appetite, which they feel pleasure in satisfying. They must propagate their respective species; an absolute necessity which proves the wisdom of the Creator, since without reproduction all would, be annihilated—by the constant law of degradation, decay and death. And, whatever St. Augustine may say, human creatures would not perform the work of generation if they did not find pleasure in it, and if there was not in that great work an irresistible attraction for them. In the third place, all creatures have a determined and invincible propensity to destroy their enemies; and it is certainly a very wise ordination, for that feeling of self-preservation makes it a duty for them to do their best for the destruction of whatever can injure them.

Each species obeys these laws in its own way. The three sensations: hunger, desire, and hatred—are in animals the satisfaction of habitual instinct, and cannot be called pleasures, for they can be so only in proportion to the intelligence of the individual. Man alone is gifted with the perfect organs which render real pleasure peculiar to him; because, being, endowed with the sublime faculty of reason, he foresees enjoyment, looks for it, composes, improves, and increases it by thought and recollection. I entreat you, dear reader, not to get weary of following me in my ramblings; for now that I am but the shadow of the once brilliant Casanova, I love to chatter; and if you were to give me the slip, you would be neither polite nor obliging.

Man comes down to the level of beasts whenever he gives himself up to the three natural propensities without calling reason and judgment to his assistance; but when the mind gives perfect equilibrium to those propensities, the sensations derived from them become true enjoyment, an unaccountable feeling which gives us what is called happiness, and which we experience without being able to describe it.

The voluptuous man who reasons, disdains greediness, rejects with contempt lust and lewdness, and spurns the brutal revenge which is caused by a first movement of anger: but he is dainty, and satisfies his appetite only in a manner in harmony with his nature and his tastes; he is amorous, but he enjoys himself with the object of his love only when he is certain that she will share his enjoyment, which can never be the case unless their love is mutual; if he is offended, he does not care for revenge until he has calmly considered the best means to enjoy it fully. If he is sometimes more cruel than necessary, he consoles himself with the idea that he has acted under the empire of reason; and his revenge is sometimes so noble that he finds it in forgiveness. Those three operations are the work of the soul which, to procure enjoyment for itself, becomes the agent of our passions. We sometimes suffer from hunger in order to enjoy better the food which will allay it; we delay the amorous enjoyment for the sake of making it more intense, and we put off the moment of our revenge in order to mike it more certain. It is true, however, that one may die from indigestion, that we allow ourselves to be often deceived in love, and that the creature we want to annihilate often escapes our revenge; but perfection cannot be attained in anything, and those are risks which we run most willingly.

CHAPTER XVII

Continuation of the Last Chapter—My First Assignation With M.   M.—Letter From C. C.—My Second Meeting With the Nun At My Splendid Casino   In Venice I Am Happy

There is nothing, there can be nothing, dearer to a thinking being than life; yet the voluptuous men, those who try to enjoy it in the best manner, are the men who practise with the greatest perfection the difficult art of shortening life, of driving it fast. They do not mean to make it shorter, for they would like to perpetuate it in the midst of pleasure, but they wish enjoyment to render its course insensible; and they are right, provided they do not fail in fulfilling their duties. Man must not, however, imagine that he has no other duties but those which gratify his senses; he would be greatly mistaken, and he might fall the victim of his own error. I think that my friend Horace made a mistake when he said to Florus:

'Nec metuam quid de me judicet heres, Quod non plura datis inveniet.'

The happiest man is the one who knows how to obtain the greatest sum of happiness without ever failing in the discharge of his duties, and the most unhappy is the man who has adopted a profession in which he finds himself constantly under the sad necessity of foreseeing the future.

Perfectly certain that M—— M—— would keep her word, I went to the convent at ten o'clock in the morning, and she joined me in the parlour as soon as I was announced.

"Good heavens!" she exclaimed, "are you ill?"

"No, but I may well look so, for the expectation of happiness wears me out. I have lost sleep and appetite, and if my felicity were to be deferred my life would be the forfeit."

"There shall be no delay, dearest; but how impatient you are! Let us sit down. Here is the key of my casino. You will find some persons in it, because we must be served; but nobody will speak to you, and you need not speak to anyone. You must be masked, and you must not go there till two hours after sunset; mind, not before. Then go up the stairs opposite the street-door, and at the top of those stairs you will see, by the light of a lamp, a green door which you will open to enter the apartment which you will find lighted. You will find me in the second room, and in case I should not be there you will wait for me a few minutes; you may rely upon my being punctual. You can take off your mask in that room, and make yourself comfortable; you will find some books and a good fire."

The description could not be clearer; I kissed the hand which was giving me the key of that mysterious temple, and I enquired from the charming woman whether I should see her in her conventual garb.

"I always leave the convent with it," she said, "but I have at the casino a complete wardrobe to transform myself into an elegant woman of the world, and even to disguise myself."

"I hope you will do me the favour to remain in the dress of a nun."

"Why so, I beg?"

"I love to see you in that dress."

"Ah! ah! I understand. You fancy that my head is shaved, and you are afraid. But comfort yourself, dear friend, my wig is so beautifully made that it defies detection; it is nature itself."

"Oh, dear! what are you saying? The very name of wig is awful. But no, you may be certain that I will find you lovely under all circumstances. I only entreat you not to put on that cruel wig in my presence. Do I offend you? Forgive me; I am very sorry to have mentioned that subject. Are you sure that no one can see you leave the convent?"

"You will be sure of it yourself when you have gone round the island and seen the small door on the shore. I have the key of a room opening on the shore, and I have every confidence in the sister who serves me."

"And the gondola?"

"My lover himself answers for the fidelity of the gondoliers."

"What a man that lover is! I fancy he must be an old man."

"You are mistaken; if he were old, I should be ashamed. He is not forty, and he has everything necessary to be loved—beauty, wit, sweet temper, and noble behaviour."

"And he forgives your amorous caprices?"

"What do you mean by caprices? A year ago he obtained possession of me, and before him I had never belonged to a man; you are the first who inspired me with a fancy. When I confessed it to him he was rather surprised, then he laughed, and read me a short lecture upon the risk I was running in trusting a man who might prove indiscreet. He wanted me to know at least who you were before going any further, but it was too late. I answered for your discretion, and of course I made him laugh by my being so positively the guarantee of a man whom I did not know."

"When did you confide in him?"

"The day before yesterday, and without concealing anything from him. I have shewn him my letters and yours; he thinks you are a Frenchman, although you represent yourself as a Venetian. He is very curious to know who you are, but you need not be afraid; I promise you faithfully never to take any steps to find it out myself."

"And I promise you likewise not to try to find out who is this wonderful man as wonderful as you are yourself. I am very miserable when I think of the sorrow I have caused you."

"Do not mention that subject any more; when I consider the matter, I see that only a conceited man would have acted differently."

Before leaving her, she granted me another token of her affection through the little window, and her gaze followed me as far as the door.

In the evening, at the time named by her, I repaired to the casino, and obeying all her instructions I reached a sitting-room in which I found my new conquest dressed in a most elegant costume. The room was lighted up by girandoles, which were reflected by the looking-glasses, and by four splendid candlesticks placed on a table covered with books. M—— M—— struck me as entirely different in her beauty to what she had seemed in the garb of a nun. She wore no cap, and her hair was fastened behind in a thick twist; but I passed rapidly over that part of her person, because I could not bear the idea of a wig, and I could not compliment her about it. I threw myself at her feet to shew her my deep gratitude, and I kissed with rapture her beautiful hands, waiting impatiently for the amorous contest which I was longing for; but M—— M—— thought fit to oppose some resistance. Oh, how sweet they are! those denials of a loving mistress, who delays the happy moment only for the sake of enjoying its delights better! As a lover respectful, tender, but bold, enterprising, certain of victory, I blended delicately the gentleness of my proceedings with the ardent fire which was consuming me; and stealing the most voluptuous kisses from the most beautiful mouth I felt as if my soul would burst from my body. We spent two hours in the preliminary contest, at the end of which we congratulated one another, on her part for having contrived to resist, on mine for having controlled my impatience.

Wanting a little rest, and understanding each other as if by a natural instinct, she said to me,

"My friend, I have an appetite which promises to do honour to the supper; are you able to keep me good company?"

"Yes," I said, knowing well what I could do in that line, "yes, I can; and afterwards you shall judge whether I am able to sacrifice to Love as well as to Comus."

She rang the bell, and a woman, middle-aged but well-dressed and respectable-looking, laid out a table for two persons; she then placed on another table close by all that was necessary to enable us to do without attendance, and she brought, one after the other, eight different dishes in Sevres porcelain placed on silver heaters. It was a delicate and plentiful supper.

When I tasted the first dish I at once recognized the French style of cooking, and she did not deny it. We drank nothing but Burgundy and Champagne. She dressed the salad cleverly and quickly, and in everything she did I had to admire the graceful ease of her manners. It was evident that she owed her education to a lover who was a first-rate connoisseur. I was curious to know him, and as we were drinking some punch I told her that if she would gratify my curiosity in that respect I was ready to tell her my name.

"Let time, dearest," she answered, "satisfy our mutual curiosity."

M—— M—— had, amongst the charms and trinkets fastened to the chain of her watch, a small crystal bottle exactly similar to one that I wore myself. I called her attention to that fact, and as mine was filled with cotton soaked in otto of roses I made her smell it.

"I have the same," she observed.

And she made me inhale its fragrance.

"It is a very scarce perfume," I said, "and very expensive."

"Yes; in fact it cannot be bought."

"Very true; the inventor of that essence wears a crown; it is the King of France; his majesty made a pound of it, which cost him thirty thousand crowns."

"Mine was a gift presented to my lover, and he gave it to me:"

"Madame de Pompadour sent a small phial of it to M. de Mocenigo, the Venetian ambassador in Paris, through M. de B——, now French ambassador here."

"Do you know him?"

"I have had the honour to dine with him on the very day he came to take leave of the ambassador by whom I had been invited. M. de B—— is a man whom fortune has smiled upon, but he has captivated it by his merit; he is not less distinguished by his 'talents than by his birth; he is, I believe, Count de Lyon. I recollect that he was nicknamed 'Belle Babet,' on account of his handsome face. There is a small collection of poetry written by him which does him great honour."

It was near midnight; we had made an excellent supper, and we were near a good fire. Besides, I was in love with a beautiful woman, and thinking that time was precious—I became very pressing; but she resisted.

"Cruel darling, have you promised me happiness only to make me suffer the tortures of Tantalus? If you will not give way to love, at least obey the laws of nature after such a delicious supper, go to bed."

"Are you sleepy?"

"Of course I am not; but it is late enough to go to bed. Allow me to undress you; I will remain by your bedside, or even go away if you wish it."

"If you were to leave me, you would grieve me."

"My grief would be as great as yours, believe me, but if I remain what shall we do?"

"We can lie down in our clothes on this sofa."

"With our clothes! Well, let it be so; I will let you sleep, if you wish it; but you must forgive me if I do not sleep myself; for to sleep near you and without undressing would be impossible."

"Wait a little."

She rose from her seat, turned the sofa crosswise, opened it, took out pillows, sheets, blankets, and in one minute we had a splendid bed, wide and convenient. She took a large handkerchief, which she wrapped round my head, and she gave me another, asking me to render her the same service. I began my task, dissembling my disgust for the wig, but a precious discovery caused me the most agreeable surprise; for, instead of the wig, my hands found the most magnificent hair I had ever seen. I uttered a scream of delight and admiration which made her laugh, and she told me that a nun was under no other obligation than to conceal her hair, from the uninitiated. Thereupon she pushed me adroitly, and made me fall' an the sofa. I got up again, and, having thrown off my clothes as quick as lightning I threw myself on her rather than near her. She was very strong; and folding me in her arms she thought that I ought to forgive her for all the torture she was condemning me to. I had not obtained any essential favour; I was burning, but I was trying to master my impatience, for I did not think that I had yet the right to be exacting. I contrived to undo five or six bows of ribbons, and satisfied, with her not opposing any resistance in that quarter my heart throbbed with pleasure, and I possessed myself of the most beautiful bosom, which I smothered under my kisses. But her favours went no further; and my excitement increasing in proportion to the new perfections I discovered in her, I doubled my efforts; all in vain. At last, compelled to give way to fatigue, I fell asleep in her arms, holding her tightly, against me. A noisy chime of bells woke us.

"What is the matter?" I exclaimed.

"Let us get up, dearest; it is time for me to return to the convent."

"Dress yourself, and let me have the pleasure of seeing you in the garb of a saint, since you are going away a virgin."

"Be satisfied for this time, dearest, and learn from me how to practice abstinence; we shall be happier another time. When I have gone, if you have nothing to hurry you, you can rest here."

She rang the bell, and the same woman who had appeared in the evening, and was most likely the secret minister and the confidante of her amorous mysteries, came in. After her hair had been dressed, she took off her gown, locked up her jewellery in her bureau, put on the stays of a nun, in which she hid the two magnificent globes which had been during that fatiguing night the principal agents of my happiness, and assumed her monastic robes. The woman having gone out to call the gondoliers, M——M—— kissed me warmly and tenderly, and said to me,

"I expect to see you the day after to-morrow, so as to hear from you which night I am to meet you in Venice; and then, my beloved lover, you shall be happy and I too. Farewell."

Pleased without being satisfied, I went to bed and slept soundly until noon.

I left the casino without seeing anyone, and being well masked I repaired to the house of Laura, who gave me a letter from my dear C—— C——. Here is a copy of it:

"I am going to give you, my best beloved, a specimen of my way of thinking; and I trust that, far from lowering me in your estimation, you will judge me, in spite of my youth, capable of keeping a secret and worthy of being your wife. Certain that your heart is mine, I do not blame you for having made a mystery of certain things, and not being jealous of what can divert your mind and help you to bear patiently our cruel separation, I can only delight in whatever procures you some pleasure. Listen now. Yesterday, as I was going along one of the halls, I dropped a tooth-pick which I held in my hand, and to get it again, I was compelled to displace a stool which happened to be in front of a crack in the partition. I have already become as curious as a nun—a fault very natural to idle people—I placed my eye against the small opening, and whom did I see? You in person, my darling, conversing in the most lively manner with my charming friend, Sister M—— M——. It would be difficult for you to imagine my surprise and joy. But those two feelings gave way soon to the fear of being seen and of exciting the curiosity of some inquisitive nun. I quickly replaced the stool, and I went away. Tell me all, dearest friend, you will make me happy. How could I cherish you with all my soul, and not be anxious to know the history of your adventure? Tell me if she knows you, and how you have made her acquaintance. She is my best friend, the one of whom I have spoken so often to you in my letters, without thinking it necessary to tell you her name. She is the friend who teaches me French, and has lent me books which gave me a great deal of information on a matter generally little known to women. If it had not been for her, the cause of the accident which has been so near costing me my life, would have been discovered. She gave me sheets and linen immediately; to her I owe my honour; but she has necessarily learned in that way that I have a lover, as I know that she has one; but neither of us has shewn any anxiety to know the secrets of the other. Sister M——

M—— is a rare woman. I feel certain, dearest, that you love one another; it cannot be otherwise since you are acquainted; but as I am not jealous of that affection, I deserve that you should tell me all. I pity you both, however; for all you may do will, I fear, only irritate your passion. Everyone in the convent thinks that you are ill, and I am longing to see you. Come, at least, once. Adieu!"

The letter of C—— C—— inspired me with the deepest esteem for her, but it caused me great anxiety, because, although I felt every confidence in my dear little wife, the small crack in the wall might expose M—— M—— and myself to the inquisitive looks of other persons. Besides, I found myself compelled to deceive that amiable, trusting friend, and to tell a falsehood, for delicacy and honour forbade me to tell her the truth. I wrote to her immediately that her friendship for M—— M—— made it her duty to warn her friend at once that she had seen her in the parlour with a masked gentleman. I added that, having heard a great deal of M—— M——'s merit, and wishing to make her acquaintance, I had called on her under an assumed name; that I entreated her not to tell her friend who I was, but she might say that she had recognized in me the gentleman who attended their church. I assured her with barefaced impudence that there was no love between M—— M—— and me, but without concealing that I thought her a superior woman.

On St. Catherine's Day, the patroness of my dear C—— C——, I bethought myself of affording that lovely prisoner the pleasure of seeing me. As I was leaving the church after mass, and just as I was going to take a gondola, I observed that a man was following me. It looked suspicious, and I determined to ascertain whether I was right. The man took a gondola and followed mine. It might have been purely accidental; but, keeping on my guard for fear of surprise, I alighted in Venice at the Morosini Palace; the fellow alighted at the same place; his intentions were evident. I left the palace, and turning towards the Flanders Gate I stopped in a narrow street, took my knife in my hand, waited for the spy, seized him by the collar, and pushing him against the wall with the knife at his throat I commanded him to tell me what business he had with me. Trembling all over he would have confessed everything, but unluckily someone entered the street. The spy escaped and I was no wiser, but I had no doubt that for the future that fellow at least would keep at a respectful distance. It shewed me how easy it would be for an obstinate spy to discover my identity, and I made up my mind never to go to Muran but with a mask, or at night.

The next day I had to see my beautiful nun in order to ascertain which day she would sup with me in Venice, and I went early to the convent. She did not keep me waiting, and her face was radiant with joy. She complimented me upon my having resumed my attendance at their church; all the nuns had been delighted to see me again after an absence of three weeks.

"The abbess," she said, "told me how glad she was to see you, and that she was certain to find out who you are."

I then related to her the adventure of the spy, and we both thought that it was most likely the means taken by the sainted woman to gratify her curiosity about me.

"I have resolved not to attend your church any more."

"That will be a great deprivation to me, but in our common interest I can but approve your resolution."

She related the affair of the treacherous crack in the partition, and added,

"It is already repaired, and there is no longer any fear in that quarter. I heard of it from a young boarder whom I love dearly, and who is much attached to me. I am not curious to know her name, and she has never mentioned it to me."

"Now, darling angel, tell me whether my happiness will be postponed."

"Yes, but only for twenty-four hours; the new professed sister has invited me to supper in her room, and you must understand I cannot invent any plausible excuse for refusing her invitation."

"You would not, then, tell her in confidence the very legitimate obstacle which makes me wish that the new sisters never take supper?"

"Certainly not: we never trust anyone so far in a convent. Besides, dearest, such an invitation cannot be declined unless I wish to gain a most bitter enemy."

"Could you not say that you are ill?"

"Yes; but then the visits!"

"I understand; if you should refuse, the escape might be suspected."

"The escape! impossible; here no one admits the possibility of breaking out of the convent."

"Then you are the only one able to perform that miracle?"

"You may be sure of that; but, as is always the case, it is gold which performs that miracle."

"And many others, perhaps."

"Oh! the time has gone by for them! But tell me, my love, where will you wait for me to-morrow, two hours after the setting of the sun?"

"Could I not wait for you at your casino?"

"No, because my lover will take me himself to Venice."

"Your lover?"

"Yes, himself."

"It is not possible."

"Yet it is true."

"I can wait for you in St. John and St. Paul's Square behind the pedestal of the statue of Bartholomew of Bergamo."

"I have never seen either the square or the statue except in engravings; it is enough, however, and I will not fail. Nothing but very stormy weather could prevent me from coming to a rendezvous for which my heart is panting."

"And if the weather were bad?"

"Then, dearest, there would be nothing lost; and you would come here again in order to appoint another day."

I had no time to lose, for I had no casino. I took a second rower so as to reach St. Mark's Square more rapidly, and I immediately set to work looking for what I wanted. When a mortal is so lucky as to be in the good graces of the god Plutus, and is not crackbrained, he is pretty sure to succeed in everything: I had not to search very long before I found a casino suiting my purpose exactly. It was the finest in the neighbourhood of Venice, but, as a natural consequence, it was likewise the most expensive. It had belonged to the English ambassador, who had sold it cheap to his cook before leaving Venice. The owner let it to me until Easter for one hundred sequins, which I paid in advance on condition that he would himself cook the dinners and the suppers I might order.

I had five rooms furnished in the most elegant style, and everything seemed to be calculated for love, pleasure, and good cheer. The service of the dining-room was made through a sham window in the wall, provided with a dumb-waiter revolving upon itself, and fitting the window so exactly that master and servants could not see each other. The drawing-room was decorated with magnificent looking-glasses, crystal chandeliers, girandoles in gilt, bronze, and with a splendid pier-glass placed on a chimney of white marble; the walls were covered with small squares of real china, representing little Cupids and naked amorous couples in all sorts of positions, well calculated to excite the imagination; elegant and very comfortable sofas were placed on every side. Next to it was an octagonal room, the walls, the ceiling, and the floor of which were entirely covered with splendid Venetian glass, arranged in such a manner as to reflect on all sides every position of the amorous couple enjoying the pleasures of love. Close by was a beautiful alcove with two secret outlets; on the right, an elegant dressing-room, on the left, a boudoir which seemed to have been arranged by the mother of Love, with a bath in Carrara marble. Everywhere the wainscots were embossed in ormolu or painted with flowers and arabesques.

After I had given my orders for all the chandeliers to be filled with wax candles, and the finest linen to be provided wherever necessary, I ordered a most delicate and sumptuous supper for two, without regard to expense, and especially the most exquisite wines. I then took possession of the key of the principal entrance, and warned the master that I did not want to be seen by anyone when I came in or went out.

I observed with pleasure that the clock in the alcove had an alarum, for I was beginning, in spite of love, to be easily influenced by the power of sleep.

Everything being arranged according to my wishes, I went, as a careful and delicate lover, to purchase the finest slippers I could find, and a cap in Alencon point.

I trust my reader does not think me too particular; let him recollect that I was to receive the most accomplished of the sultanas of the master of the universe, and I told that fourth Grace that I had a casino. Was I to begin by giving her a bad idea of my truthfulness? At the appointed time, that is two hours after sunset, I repaired to my palace; and it would be difficult to imagine the surprise of his honour the French cook, when he saw me arrive alone. Not finding all the chandeliers lighted-up as I had ordered, I scolded him well, giving him notice that I did not like to repeat an order.

"I shall not fail; sir, another time, to execute your commands."

"Let the supper be served."

"Your honour ordered it for two."

"Yes, for two; and, this time, be present during my supper, so that I can tell you which dishes I find good or bad."

The supper came through the revolving: dumb-waiter in very good order, two dishes at a time. I passed some remarks upon everything; but, to tell the truth, everything was excellent: game, fish, oysters, truffles, wine, dessert, and the whole served in very fine Dresden china and silver-gilt plate.

I told him that he had forgotten hard eggs, anchovies, and prepared vinegar to dress a salad. He lifted his eyes towards heaven, as if to plead guilty, to a very heinous crime.

After a supper which lasted two hours, and during which I must certainly have won the admiration of my host, I asked him to bring me the bill. He presented it to me shortly afterwards, and I found it reasonable. I then dismissed him, and lay down in the splendid bed in the alcove; my excellent supper brought on very soon the most delicious sleep which, without the Burgundy and the Champagne, might very likely not have visited me, if I had thought that the following night would see me in the same place, and in possession of a lovely divinity. It was broad day-light when I awoke, and after ordering the finest fruit and some ices for the evening I left the casino. In order to shorten a day which my impatient desires would have caused me to find very long, I went to the faro-table, and I saw with pleasure that I was as great a favourite with fortune as with love. Everything proceeded according to my wishes, and I delighted in ascribing my happy success to the influence of my nun.

I was at the place of meeting one hour before the time appointed, and although the night was cold I did not feel it. Precisely as the hour struck I saw a two-oared gondola reach the shore and a mask come out of it, speak a few words to the gondolier, and take the direction of the statue. My heart was beating quickly, but seeing that it was a man I avoided him, and regretted not having brought my pistols. The mask, however, turning round the statue, came up to me with outstretched hands; I then recognized my angel, who was amused at my surprise and took my arm. Without speaking we went towards St. Mark's Square, and reached my casino, which was only one hundred yards from the St. Moses Theatre.

I found everything in good order; we went upstairs and I threw off my mask and my disguise; but M—— M—— took delight in walking about the rooms and in examining every nook of the charming place in which she was received. Highly gratified to see me admire the grace of her person, she wanted me likewise to admire in her attire the taste and generosity of her lover. She was surprised at the almost magic spell which, although she remained motionless, shewed her lovely person in a thousand different manners. Her multiplied portraits, reproduced by the looking-glasses, and the numerous wax candles disposed to that effect, offered to her sight a spectacle entirely new to her, and from which she could not withdraw her eyes. Sitting down on a stool I contemplated her elegant person with rapture. A coat of rosy velvet, embroidered with gold spangles, a vest to match, embroidered likewise in the richest fashion, breeches of black satin, diamond buckles, a solitaire of great value on her little finger, and on the other hand a ring: such was her toilet. Her black lace mask was remarkable for its fineness and the beauty of the design. To enable me to see her better she stood before me. I looked in her pockets, in which I found a gold snuff-box, a sweetmeat-box adorned with pearls, a gold case, a splendid opera-glass, handkerchiefs of the finest cambric, soaked rather than perfumed with the most precious essences. I examined attentively the richness and the workmanship of her two watches, of her chains, of her trinkets, brilliant with diamonds. The last article I found was a pistol; it was an English weapon of fine steel, and of the most beautiful finish.

"All I see, my divine angel, is not worthy of you; yet I cannot refrain from expressing my admiration for the wonderful, I might almost say adorable, being who wants to convince you that you are truly his mistress."

"That is what he said when I asked him to bring me to Venice, and to leave me. 'Amuse yourself,' he said, 'and I hope that the man whom you are going to make happy will convince you that he is worthy of it.'"

"He is indeed an extraordinary man, and I do not think there is another like him. Such a lover is a unique being; and I feel that I could not be like him, as deeply as I fear to be unworthy of a happiness which dazzles me."

"Allow me to leave you, and to take off these clothes alone."

"Do anything you please."

A quarter of an hour afterwards my mistress came back to me. Her hair was dressed like a man's; the front locks came down her cheeks, and the black hair, fastened with a knot of blue ribbon, reached the bend of her legs; her form was that of Antinous; her clothes alone, being cut in the French style, prevented the illusion from being complete. I was in a state of ecstatic delight, and I could not realize my happiness.

"No, adorable woman," I exclaimed, "you are not made for a mortal, and I do not believe that you will ever be mine. At the very moment of possessing you some miracle will wrest you from my arms. Your divine spouse, perhaps, jealous of a simple mortal, will annihilate all my hope. It is possible that in a few minutes I shall no longer exist."

"Are you mad, dearest? I am yours this very instant, if you wish it."

"Ah! if I wish it! Although fasting, come! Love and happiness will be my food!"

She felt cold, we sat near the fire; and unable to master my impatience I unfastened a diamond brooch which pinned her ruffle. Dear reader, there are some sensations so powerful and so sweet that years cannot weaken the remembrance of them. My mouth had already covered with kisses that ravishing bosom; but then the troublesome corset had not allowed me to admire all its perfection. Now I felt it free from all restraint and from all unnecessary support; I have never seen, never touched, anything more beautiful, and the two magnificent globes of the Venus de Medicis, even if they had been animated by the spark of life given by Prometheus, would have yielded the palm to hose of my divine nun.

I was burning with ardent desires, and I would have satisfied them on the spot, if my adorable mistress had not calmed my impatience by these simple words:

"Wait until after supper."

I rang the bell; she shuddered.

"Do not be anxious, dearest."

And I shewed her the secret of the sham window.

"You will be able to tell your lover that no one saw you."

"He will appreciate your delicate attention, and that will prove to him that you are not a novice in the art of love. But it is evident that I am not the only one who enjoys with you the delights of this charming residence."

"You are wrong, believe me: you are the first woman I have seen here. You are not, adorable creature, my first love, but you shall be the last."

"I shall be happy if you are faithful. My lover is constant, kind, gentle and amiable; yet my heart has ever been fancy-free with him."

"Then his own heart must be the same; for if his love was of the same nature as mine you would never have made me happy."

"He loves me as I love you; do you believe in my love for you?"

"Yes, I want to believe in it; but you would not allow me to...."

"Do not say any more; for I feel that I could forgive you in anything, provided you told me all. The joy I experience at this moment is caused more by the hope I have of gratifying your desires than by the idea that I am going to pass a delightful night with you. It will be the first in my life."

"What! Have you never passed such a night with your lover?"

"Several; but friendship, compliance, and gratitude, perhaps, were then the only contributors to our pleasures; the most essential— love—was never present. In spite of that, my lover is like you; his wit is lively, very much the same as yours, and, as far as his features are concerned, he is very handsome; yet it is not you. I believe him more wealthy than you, although this casino almost convinces me that I am mistaken, but what does love care for riches? Do not imagine that I consider you endowed with less merit than he, because you confess yourself incapable of his heroism in allowing me to enjoy another love. Quite the contrary; I know that you would not love me as you do, if you told me that you could be as indulgent as he is for one of my caprices."

"Will he be curious to hear the particulars of this night?"

"Most likely he will think that he will please me by asking what has taken place, and I will tell him everything, except such particulars as might humiliate him."

After the supper, which she found excellent, she made some punch, and she was a very good hand at it. But I felt my impatience growing stronger every moment, and I said,

"Recollect that we have only seven hours before us, and that we should be very foolish to waste them in this room."

"You reason better than Socrates," she answered, "and your eloquence has convinced me. Come!"

She led me to the elegant dressing-room, and I offered her the fine night-cap which I had bought for her, asking her at the same time to dress her hair like a woman. She took it with great pleasure, and begged me to go and undress myself in the drawing-room, promising to call me as soon as she was in bed.

I had not long to wait: when pleasure is waiting for us, we all go quickly to work. I fell into her arms, intoxicated with love and happiness, and during seven hours I gave her the most positive proofs of my ardour and of the feelings I entertained for her. It is true that she taught me nothing new, materially speaking, but a great deal in sighs, in ecstasies, in enjoyments which can have their full development only in a sensitive soul in the sweetest of all moments. I varied our pleasures in a thousand different ways, and I astonished her by making her feel that she was susceptible of greater enjoyment than she had any idea of. At last the fatal alarum was heard: we had to stop our amorous transports; but before she left my arms she raised her eyes towards heaven as if to thank her Divine Master for having given her the courage to declare her passion to me.

We dressed ourselves, and observing that I put the lace night-cap in her pocket she assured me that she would keep it all her life as a witness of the happiness which overwhelmed her. After drinking a cup of coffee we went out, and I left her at St. John and St. Paul's Square, promising to call on her the day after the morrow; I watched her until I saw her safe in her gondola, and I then went to bed. Ten hours of profound sleep restored me to my usual state of vigour.

CHAPTER XVIII

Visit to the Convent and Conversation With M. M.—A Letter from Her, and
My Answer—Another Interview At the Casino of Muran In the Presence of
Her Lover

According to my promise, I went to see M—— M—— two days afterwards, but as soon as she came to the parlour she told me that her lover had said he was coming, and that she expected him every minute, and that she would be glad to see me the next day. I took leave of her, but near the bridge I saw a man, rather badly masked, coming out of a gondola. I looked at the gondolier, and I recognized him as being in the service of the French ambassador. "It is he," I said to myself, and without appearing to observe him I watched him enter the convent. I had no longer any doubt as to his identity, and I returned to Venice delighted at having made the discovery, but I made up my mind not to say anything to my mistress.

I saw her on the following day, and we, had a long conversation together, which I am now going to relate.

"My friend," she said to me, "came yesterday in order to bid farewell to me until the Christmas holidays. He is going to Padua, but everything has been arranged so that we can sup at his casino whenever we wish."

"Why not in Venice?"

"He has begged me not to go there during his absence. He is wise and prudent; I could not refuse his request."

"You are quite right. When shall we sup together?"

"Next Sunday, if you like."

"If I like is not the right expression, for I always like. On Sunday, then, I will go to the casino towards nightfall, and wait for you with a book. Have you told your friend that you were not very uncomfortable in my small palace?"

"He knows all about it, but, dearest, he is afraid of one thing—he fears a certain fatal plumpness...."

"On my life, I never thought of that! But, my darling, do you not run the same risk with him?"

"No, it is impossible."

"I understand you. Then we must be very prudent for the future. I believe that, nine days before Christmas, the mask is no longer allowed, and then I shall have to go to your casino by water, otherwise, I might easily be recognized by the same spy who has already followed me once."

"Yes, that idea proves your prudence, and I can easily, shew you the place. I hope you will be able to come also during Lent, although we are told that at that time God wishes us to mortify our senses. Is it not strange that there is a time during which God wants us to amuse ourselves almost to frenzy, and another during which, in order to please Him, we must live in complete abstinence? What is there in common between a yearly observance and the Deity, and how can the action of the creature have any influence over the Creator, whom my reason cannot conceive otherwise than independent? It seems to me that if God had created man with the power of offending Him, man would be right in doing everything that is forbidden to him, because the deficiencies of his organization would be the work of the Creator Himself. How can we imagine God grieved during Lent?"

"My beloved one, you reason beautifully, but will you tell me where you have managed, in a convent, to pass the Rubicon?"

"Yes. My friend has given me some good books which I have read with deep attention, and the light of truth has dispelled the darkness which blinded my eyes. I can assure you that, when I look in my own heart, I find myself more fortunate in having met with a person who has brought light to my mind than miserable at having taken the veil; for the greatest happiness must certainly consist in living and in dying peacefully—a happiness which can hardly be obtained by listening to all the idle talk with which the priests puzzle our brains."

"I am of your opinion, but I admire you, for it ought to be the work of more than a few months to bring light to a mind prejudiced as yours was."

"There is no doubt that I should have seen light much sooner if I had not laboured under so many prejudices. There was in my mind a curtain dividing truth from error, and reason alone could draw it aside, but that poor reason—I had been taught to fear it, to repulse it, as if its bright flame would have devoured, instead of enlightening me. The moment it was proved to me that a reasonable being ought to be guided only by his own inductions I acknowledged the sway of reason, and the mist which hid truth from me was dispelled. The evidence of truth shone before my eyes, nonsensical trifles disappeared, and I have no fear of their resuming their influence over my mind, for every day it is getting stronger; and I may say that I only began to love God when my mind was disabused of priestly superstitions concerning Him."

"I congratulate you; you have been more fortunate than I, for you have made more progress in one year than I have made in ten."

"Then you did not begin by reading the writings of Lord Bolingbroke? Five or six months ago, I was reading La Sagesse, by Charron, and somehow or other my confessor heard of it; when I went to him for confession, he took upon himself to tell me to give up reading that book. I answered that my conscience did not reproach me, and that I could not obey him. 'In that case,' replied he, 'I will not give you absolution.' 'That will not prevent me from taking the communion,' I said. This made him angry, and, in order to know what he ought to do, he applied to Bishop Diedo. His eminence came to see me, and told me that I ought to be guided by my confessor. I answered that we had mutual duties to perform, and that the mission of a priest in the confessional was to listen to me, to impose a reasonable penance, and to give me absolution; that he had not even the right of offering me any advice if I did not ask for it. I added that the confessor being bound to avoid scandal, if he dared to refuse me the absolution, which, of course, he could do, I would all the same go to the altar with the other nuns. The bishop, seeing that he was at his wit's end, told the priest to abandon me to my conscience. But that was not satisfactory to me, and my lover obtained a brief from the Pope authorizing me to go to confession to any priest I like. All the sisters are jealous of the privilege, but I have availed myself of it only once, for the sake of establishing a precedent and of strengthening the right by the fact, for it is not worth the trouble. I always confess to the same priest, and he has no difficulty in giving me absolution, for I only tell him what I like."

"And for the rest you absolve yourself?"

"I confess to God, who alone can know my thoughts and judge the degree of merit or of demerit to be attached to my actions."

Our conversation shewed me that my lovely friend was what is called a Free-thinker; but I was not astonished at it, because she felt a greater need of peace for her conscience than of gratification for her senses.

On the Sunday, after dinner, I took a two-oared gondola, and went round the island of Muran to reconnoitre the shore, and to discover the small door through which my mistress escaped from the convent. I lost my trouble and my time, for I did not become acquainted with the shore till the octave of Christmas, and with the small door six months afterwards. I shall mention the circumstance in its proper place.

As soon as it was time, I repaired to the temple, and while I was waiting for the idol I amused myself in examining the books of a small library in the boudoir. They were not numerous, but they were well chosen and worthy of the place. I found there everything that has been written against religion, and all the works of the most voluptuous writers on pleasure; attractive books, the incendiary style of which compels the reader to seek the reality of the image they represent. Several folios, richly bound, contained nothing but erotic engravings. Their principal merit consisted much more in the beauty of the designs, in the finish of the work, than in the lubricity of the positions. I found amongst them the prints of the Portier des Chartreux, published in England; the engravings of Meursius, of Aloysia Sigea Toletana, and others, all very beautifully done. A great many small pictures covered the walls of the boudoir, and they were all masterpieces in the same style as the engravings.

I had spent an hour in examining all these works of art, the sight of which had excited me in the most irresistible manner, when I saw my beautiful mistress enter the room, dressed as a nun. Her appearance was not likely to act as a sedative, and therefore, without losing any time in compliments, I said to her,

"You arrive most opportunely. All these erotic pictures have fired my imagination, and it is in your garb of a saint that you must administer the remedy that my love requires."

"Let me put on another dress, darling, it will not take more than five minutes."

"Five minutes will complete my happiness, and then you can attend to your metamorphosis."

"But let me take off these woollen robes, which I dislike."

"No; I want you to receive the homage of my love in the same dress which you had on when you gave birth to it."

She uttered in the humblest manner a 'fiat voluntas tua', accompanied by the most voluptuous smile, and sank on the sofa. For one instant we forgot all the world besides. After that delightful ecstacy I assisted her to undress, and a simple gown of Indian muslin soon metamorphosed my lovely nun into a beautiful nymph.

After an excellent supper, we agreed not to meet again till the first day of the octave. She gave me the key of the gate on the shore, and told me that a blue ribbon attached to the window over the door would point it out by day, so as to prevent my making a mistake at night. I made her very happy by telling her that I would come and reside in her casino until the return of her friend. During the ten days that I remained there, I saw her four times, and I convinced her that I lived only for her.

During my stay in the casino I amused myself in reading, in writing to C—— C——, but my love for her had become a calm affection. The lines which interested me most in her letters were those in which she mentioned her friend. She often blamed me for not having cultivated the acquaintance of M—— M——, and my answer was that I had not done so for fear of being known. I always insisted upon the necessity of discretion.

I do not believe in the possibility of equal love being bestowed upon two persons at the same time, nor do I believe it possible to keep love to a high degree of intensity if you give it either too much food or none at all. That which maintained my passion for M—— M —— in a state of great vigour was that I could never possess her without running the risk of losing her.

"It is impossible," I said to her once, "that some time or other one of the nuns should not want to speak to you when you are absent?"

"No," she answered, "that cannot happen, because there is nothing more religiously respected in a convent than the right of a nun to deny herself, even to the abbess. A fire is the only circumstance I have to fear, because in that case there would be general uproar and confusion, and it would not appear natural that a nun should remain quietly locked up in her cell in the midst of such danger; my escape would then be discovered. I have contrived to gain over the lay-sister and the gardener, as well as another nun, and that miracle was performed by my cunning assisted by my lover's gold.

"He answers for the fidelity of the cook and his wife who take care of the casino. He has likewise every confidence in the two gondoliers, although one of them is sure to be a spy of the State Inquisitors."

On Christmas Eve she announced the return of her lover, and she told him that on St. Stephen's Day she would go with him to the opera, and that they would afterwards spend the night together.

"I shall expect you, my beloved one," she added, "on the last day of the year, and here is a letter which I beg you not to read till you get home."

As I had to move in order to make room for her lover, I packed my things early in the morning, and, bidding farewell to a place in which during ten days I had enjoyed so many delights, I returned to the Bragadin Palace, where I read the following letter:

"You have somewhat offended me, my own darling, by telling me, respecting the mystery which I am bound to keep on the subject of my lover, that, satisfied to possess my heart, you left me mistress of my mind. That division of the heart and of the mind appears to me a pure sophism, and if it does not strike you as such you must admit that you do not love me wholly, for I cannot exist without mind, and you cannot cherish my heart if it does not agree with my mind. If your love cannot accept a different state of things it does not excel in delicacy. However, as some circumstance might occur in which you might accuse me of not having acted towards you with all the sincerity that true love inspires, and that it has a right to demand, I have made up my mind to confide to you a secret which concerns my friend, although I am aware that he relies entirely upon my discretion. I shall certainly be guilty of a breach of confidence, but you will not love me less for it, because, compelled to choose between you two, and to deceive either one or the other, love has conquered friendship; do not punish me for it, for it has not been done blindly, and you will, I trust, consider the reasons which have caused the scale to weigh down in your favour.

"When I found myself incapable of resisting my wish to know you and to become intimate with you, I could not gratify that wish without taking my friend into my confidence, and I had no doubt of his compliance. He conceived a very favourable opinion of your character from your first letter, not only because you had chosen the parlour of the convent for our first interview, but also because you appointed his casino at Muran instead of your own. But he likewise begged of me to allow him to be present at our first meeting-place, in a small closet—a true hiding-place, from which one can see and hear everything without being suspected by those in the drawing-room. You have not yet seen that mysterious closet, but I will shew it to you on the last day of the year. Tell me, dearest, whether I could refuse that singular request to the man who was shewing me such compliant kindness? I consented, and it was natural for me not to let you know it. You are therefore aware now that my friend was a witness of all we did and said during the first night that we spent together, but do not let that annoy you, for you pleased him in everything, in your behaviour towards me as well as in the witty sayings which you uttered to make me laugh. I was in great fear, when the conversation turned upon him, lest you would say something which might hurt his self-love, but, very fortunately, he heard only the most flattering compliments. Such is, dearest love, the sincere confession of my treason, but as a wise lover you will forgive me because it has not done you the slightest harm. My friend is extremely curious to ascertain who you are. But listen to me, that night you were natural and thoroughly amiable, would you have been the same, if you had known that there was a witness? It is not likely, and if I had acquainted you with the truth, you might have refused your consent, and perhaps you would have been right.

"Now that we know each other, and that you entertain no doubt, I trust, of my devoted love, I wish to ease my conscience and to venture all. Learn then, dearest, that on the last day of the year, my friend will be at the casino, which he will leave only the next morning. You will not see him, but he will see us. As you are supposed not to know anything about it, you must feel that you will have to be natural in everything, otherwise, he might guess that I have betrayed the secret. It is especially in your conversation that you must be careful. My friend possesses every virtue except the theological one called faith, and on that subject you can say anything you like. You will be at liberty to talk literature, travels, politics, anything you please, and you need not refrain from anecdotes. In fact you are certain of his approbation.

"Now, dearest, I have only this to say. Do you feel disposed to allow yourself to be seen by another man while you are abandoning yourself to the sweet voluptuousness of your senses? That doubt causes all my anxiety, and I entreat from you an answer, yes or no. Do you understand how painful the doubt is for me? I expect not to close my eyes throughout the night, and I shall not rest until I have your decision. In case you should object to shew your tenderness in the presence of a third person, I will take whatever determination love may suggest to me. But I hope you will consent, and even if you were not to perform the character of an ardent lover in a masterly manner, it would not be of any consequence. I will let my friend believe that your love has not reached its apogee."

That letter certainly took me by surprise, but all things considered, thinking that my part was better than the one accepted by the lover, I laughed heartily at the proposal. I confess, however, that I should not have laughed if I had not known the nature of the individual who was to be the witness of my amorous exploits. Understanding all the anxiety of my friend, and wishing to allay it, I immediately wrote to her the following lines:

"You wish me, heavenly creature, to answer you yes or no, and I, full of love for you, want my answer to reach you before noon, so that you may dine in perfect peace.

"I will spend the last night of the year with you, and I can assure you that the friend, to whom we will give a spectacle worthy of Paphos and Amathos, shall see or hear nothing likely to make him suppose that I am acquainted with his secret. You may be certain that I will play my part not as a novice but as a master. If it is man's duty to be always the slave of his reason; if, as long as he has control over himself, he ought not to act without taking it for his guide, I cannot understand why a man should be ashamed to shew himself to a friend at the very moment that he is most favoured by love and nature.

"Yet I confess that you would have been wrong if you had confided the secret to me the first time, and that most likely I should then have refused to grant you that mark of my compliance, not because I loved you less then than I do now, but there are such strange tastes in nature that I might have imagined that your lover's ruling taste was to enjoy the sight of an ardent and frantic couple in the midst of amorous connection, and in that case, conceiving an unfavourable opinion of you, vexation might have frozen the love you had just sent through my being. Now, however, the case is very different. I know all I possess in you, and, from all you have told me of your lover, I am well disposed towards him, and I believe him to be my friend. If a feeling of modesty does not deter you from shewing yourself tender, loving, and full of amorous ardour with me in his presence, how could I be ashamed, when, on the contrary, I ought to feel proud of myself? I have no reason to blush at having made a conquest of you, or at shewing myself in those moments during which I prove the liberality with which nature has bestowed upon me the shape and the strength which assure such immense enjoyment to me, besides the certainty that I can make the woman I love share it with me. I am aware that, owing to a feeling which is called natural, but which is perhaps only the result of civilization and the effect of the prejudices inherent in youth, most men object to any witness in those moments, but those who cannot give any good reasons for their repugnance must have in their nature something of the cat. At the same time, they might have some excellent reasons, without their thinking themselves bound to give them, except to the woman, who is easily deceived. I excuse with all my heart those who know that they would only excite the pity of the witnesses, but we both have no fear of that sort. All you have told me of your friend proves that he will enjoy our pleasures. But do you know what will be the result of it? The intensity of our ardour will excite his own, and he will throw himself at my feet, begging and entreating me to give up to him the only object likely to calm his amorous excitement. What could I do in that case? Give you up? I could hardly refuse to do so with good grace, but I would go away, for I could not remain a quiet spectator.

"Farewell, my darling love; all will be well, I have no doubt. Prepare yourself for the athletic contest, and rely upon the fortunate being who adores you."

I spent the six following days with my three worthy friends, and at the 'ridotto', which at that time was opened on St. Stephen's Day. As I could not hold the cards there, the patricians alone having the privilege of holding the bank, I played morning and evening, and I constantly lost; for whoever punts must lose. But the loss of the four or five thousand sequins I possessed, far from cooling my love, seemed only to increase its ardour.

At the end of the year 1774 the Great Council promulgated a law forbidding all games of chance, the first effect of which was to close the 'ridotto'. This law was a real phenomenon, and when the votes were taken out of the urn the senators looked at each other with stupefaction. They had made the law unwittingly, for three-fourths of the voters objected to it, and yet three-fourths of the votes were in favour of it. People said that it was a miracle of St. Mark's, who had answered the prayers of Monsignor Flangini, then censor-in-chief, now cardinal, and one of the three State Inquisitors.

On the day appointed I was punctual at the place of rendezvous, and I had not to wait for my mistress. She was in the dressing-room, where she had had time to attend to her toilet, and as soon as she heard me she came to me dressed with the greatest elegance.

"My friend is not yet at his post," she said to me, "but the moment he is there I will give you a wink."

"Where is the mysterious closet?"

"There it is. Look at the back of this sofa against the wall. All those flowers in relief have a hole in the centre which communicates with the closet behind that wall. There is a bed, a table, and everything necessary to a person who wants to spend the night in amusing himself by looking at what is going on in this room. I will skew it to you whenever you like."

"Was it arranged by your lover's orders?"

"No, for he could not foresee that he would use it."

"I understand that he may find great pleasure in such a sight, but being unable to possess you at the very moment nature will make you most necessary to him, what will he do?"

"That is his business. Besides, he is at liberty to go away when he has had enough of it, or to sleep if he has a mind to, but if you play your part naturally he will not feel any weariness."

"I will be most natural, but I must be more polite."

"No, no politeness, I beg, for if you are polite, goodbye to nature. Where have you ever seen, I should like to know, two lovers, excited by all the fury of love, think of politeness?"

"You are right, darling, but I must be more delicate."

"Very well, delicacy can do no harm, but no more than usual. Your letter greatly pleased me, you have treated the subject like a man of experience."

I have already stated that my mistress was dressed most elegantly, but I ought to have added that it was the elegance of the Graces, and that it did not in any way prevent ease and simplicity. I only wondered at her having used some paint for the face, but it rather pleased me because she had applied it according to the fashion of the ladies of Versailles. The charm of that style consists in the negligence with which the paint is applied. The rouge must not appear natural; it is used to please the eyes which see in it the marks of an intoxication heralding the most amorous fury. She told me that she had put some on her face to please her inquisitive friend, who was very fond of it.

"That taste," I said, "proves him to be a Frenchman."

As I was uttering these words, she made a sign to me; the friend was at his post, and now the play began.

"The more I look at you, beloved angel, the more I think you worthy of my adoration."

"But are you not certain that you do not worship a cruel divinity?"

"Yes, and therefore I do not offer my sacrifices to appease you, but to excite you. You shall feel all through the night the ardour of my devotion."

"You will not find me insensible to your offerings."

"I would begin them at once, but I think that, in order to insure their efficiency, we ought to have supper first. I have taken nothing to-day but a cup of chocolate and a salad of whites of eggs dressed with oil from Lucca and Marseilles vinegar."

"But, dearest, it is folly! you must be ill?"

"Yes, I am just now, but I shall be all right when I have distilled the whites of eggs, one by one, into your amorous soul."

"I did not think you required any such stimulants."

"Who could want any with you? But I have a rational fear, for if I happened to prime without being able to fire, I would blow my brains out."

"My dear browny, it would certainly be a misfortune, but there would be no occasion to be in despair on that account."

"You think that I would only have to prime again."

"Of course."

While we were bantering in this edifying fashion, the table had been laid, and we sat down to supper. She ate for two and I for four, our excellent appetite being excited by the delicate cheer. A sumptuous dessert was served in splendid silver-gilt plate, similar to the two candlesticks which held four wax candles each. Seeing that I admired them, she said:

"They are a present from my friend."

"It is a magnificent present, has he given you the snuffers likewise?"

"No."

"It is a proof that your friend is a great nobleman."

"How so?"

"Because great lords have no idea of snuffing the candle."

"Our candles have wicks which never require that operation."

"Good! Tell me who has taught you French."

"Old La Forest. I have been his pupil for six years. He has also taught me to write poetry, but you know a great many words which I never heard from him, such as 'a gogo, frustratoire, rater, dorloter'. Who taught you these words?"

"The good company in Paris, and women particularly."

We made some punch, and amused ourselves in eating oysters after the voluptuous fashion of lovers. We sucked them in, one by one, after placing them on the other's tongue. Voluptuous reader, try it, and tell me whether it is not the nectar of the gods!

At last, joking was over, and I reminded her that we had to think of more substantial pleasures. "Wait here," she said, "I am going to change my dress. I shall be back in one minute." Left alone, and not knowing what to do, I looked in the drawers of her writing-table. I did not touch the letters, but finding a box full of certain preservative sheaths against the fatal and dreaded plumpness, I emptied it, and I placed in it the following lines instead of the stolen goods:

'Enfants de L'Amitie, ministres de la Peur, Je suis l'Amour, tremblez, respectez le voleur! Et toi, femme de Dieu, ne crains pas d'etre mere; Car si to le deviens, Dieu seal sera le pere. S'il est dit cependant que tu veux le barren, Parle; je suis tout pret, je me ferai chatrer.'

My mistress soon returned, dressed like a nymph. A gown of Indian muslin, embroidered with gold lilies, spewed to admiration the outline of her voluptuous form, and her fine lace-cap was worthy of a queen. I threw myself at her feet, entreating her not to delay my happiness any longer.

"Control your ardour a few moments," she said, "here is the altar, and in a few minutes the victim will be in your arms."

"You will see," she added, going to her writing-table, "how far the delicacy and the kind attention of my friend can extend."

She took the box and opened it, but instead of the pretty sheaths that she expected to see, she found my poetry. After reading it aloud, she called me a thief, and smothering me with kisses she entreated me to give her back what I had stolen, but I pretended not to understand. She then read the lines again, considered for one moment, and under pretence of getting a better pen, she left the room, saying,

"I am going to pay you in your own coin."

She came back after a few minutes and wrote the following six lines:

'Sans rien oter au plaisir amoureux, L'objet de ton larcin sert a combler nos voeux. A l'abri du danger, mon ame satisfaite Savoure en surete parfaite; Et si tu veux jauer avec securite, Rends-moi mon doux ami, ces dons de l'amitie.

After this I could not resist any longer, and I gave her back those objects so precious to a nun who wants to sacrifice on the altar of Venus.

The clock striking twelve, I shewed her the principal actor who was longing to perform, and she arranged the sofa, saying that the alcove being too cold we had better sleep on it. But the true reason was that, to satisfy the curious lover, it was necessary for us to be seen.

Dear reader, a picture must have shades, and there is nothing, no matter how beautiful in one point of view, that does not require to be sometimes veiled if you look at it from a different one. In order to paint the diversified scene which took place between me and my lovely mistress until the dawn of day, I should have to use all the colours of Aretino's palette. I was ardent and full of vigour, but I had to deal with a strong partner, and in the morning, after the last exploit, we were positively worn out; so much so that my charming nun felt some anxiety on my account. It is true that she had seen my blood spurt out and cover her bosom during my last offering; and as she did not suspect the true cause of that phenomenon, she turned pale with fright. I allayed her anxiety by a thousand follies which made her laugh heartily. I washed her splendid bosom with rosewater, so as to purify it from the blood by which it had been dyed for the first time. She expressed a fear that she had swallowed a few drops, but I told her that it was of no consequence, even if were the case. She resumed the costume of a nun, and entreating me to lie down and to write to her before returning to Venice, so as to let her know how I was, she left the casino.

I had no difficulty in obeying her, for I was truly in great need of rest. I slept until evening. As soon as I awoke, I wrote to her that my health was excellent, and that I felt quite inclined to begin our delightful contest all over again. I asked her to let me know how she was herself, and after I had dispatched my letter I returned to Venice.

CHAPTER XIX

I Give My Portrait to M. M.—A Present From Her—I Go to the Opera   With Her—She Plays At the Faro Table and Replenishes My Empty Purse—Philosophical Conversation With M. M.—A Letter From C. C.—She Knows All—A Ball At the Convent; My Exploits In the Character of Pierrot—C. C. Comes to the Casino Instead of M. M.—I Spend the Night With Her In A Very Silly Way.

My dear M—— M—— had expressed a wish to have my portrait, something like the one I had given to C—— C——, only larger, to wear it as a locket. The outside was to represent some saint, and an invisible spring was to remove the sainted picture and expose my likeness. I called upon the artist who had painted the other miniature for me, and in three sittings I had what I wanted. He afterwards made me an Annunciation, in which the angel Gabriel was transformed into a dark-haired saint, and the Holy Virgin into a beautiful, light-complexioned woman holding her arms towards the angel. The celebrated painter Mengs imitated that idea in the picture of the Annunciation which he painted in Madrid twelve years afterwards, but I do not know whether he had the same reasons for it as my painter. That allegory was exactly of the same size as my portrait, and the jeweller who made the locket arranged it in such a manner that no one could suppose the sacred image to be there only for the sake of hiding a profane likeness.

The end of January, 1754, before going to the casino, I called upon Laura to give her a letter for C—— C——, and she handed me one from her which amused me. My beautiful nun had initiated that young girl, not only into the mysteries of Sappho, but also in high metaphysics, and C—— C—— had consequently become a Freethinker. She wrote to me that, objecting to give an account of her affairs to her confessor, and yet not wishing to tell him falsehoods, she had made up her mind to tell him nothing.

"He has remarked," she added, "that perhaps I do not confess anything to him because I did not examine my conscience sufficiently, and I answered him that I had nothing to say, but that if he liked I would commit a few sins for the purpose of having something to tell him in confession."

I thought this reply worthy of a thorough sophist, and laughed heartily.

On the same day I received the following letter from my adorable nun "I write to you from my bed, dearest browny, because I cannot remain standing on my feet. I am almost dead. But I am not anxious about it; a little rest will make me all right, for I eat well and sleep soundly. You have made me very happy by writing to me that your bleeding has not had any evil consequences, and I give you fair notice that I shall have the proof of it on Twelfth Night, at least if you like; that is understood, and you will let me know. In case you should feel disposed to grant me that favour, my darling, I wish to go to the opera. At all events, recollect that I positively forbid the whites of eggs for the future, for I would rather have a little less enjoyment and more security respecting your health. In future, when you go to the casino of Muran, please to enquire whether there is anybody there, and if you receive an affirmative answer, go away. My friend will do the same. In that manner you will not run the risk of meeting one another, but you need not observe these precautions for long, if you wish, for my friend is extremely fond of you, and has a great desire to make your acquaintance. He has told me that, if he had not seen it with his own eyes, he never would have believed that a man could run the race that you ran so splendidly the other night, but he says that, by making love in that manner, you bid defiance to death, for he is certain that the blood you lost comes from the brain. But what will he say when he hears that you only laugh at the occurrence? I am going to make you very merry: he wants to eat the salad of whites of eggs, and he wants me to ask you for some of your vinegar, because there is none in Venice. He said that he spent a delightful night, in spite of his fear of the evil consequences of our amorous sport, and he has found my own efforts superior to the usual weakness of my sex. That may be the case, dearest browny, but I am delighted to have done such wonders, and to have made such trial of my strength. Without you, darling of my heart, I should have lived without knowing myself, and I wonder whether it is possible for nature to create a woman who could remain insensible in your arms, or rather one who would not receive new life by your side. It is more than love that I feel for you, it is idolatry; and my mouth, longing to meet yours, sends forth thousands of kisses which are wasted in the air. I am panting for your divine portrait, so as to quench by a sweet illusion the fire which devours my amorous lips. I trust my likeness will prove equally dear to you, for it seems to me that nature has created us for one another, and I curse the fatal instant in which I raised an invincible barrier between us. You will find enclosed the key of my bureau. Open it, and take a parcel on which you will see written, 'For my darling.' It is a small present which my friend wishes me to offer you in exchange for the beautiful night-cap that you gave me. Adieu."

The small key enclosed in the letter belonged to a bureau in the boudoir. Anxious to know the nature of the present that she could offer me at the instance of her friend, I opened the bureau, and found a parcel containing a letter and a morocco-leather case.

The letter was as follows:

"That which will, I hope, render this present dear to you is the portrait of a woman who adores you. Our friend had two of them, but the great friendship he entertains towards you has given him the happy idea of disposing of one in your favour. This box contains two portraits of me, which are to be seen in two different ways: if you take off the bottom part, of the case in its length, you will see me as a nun; and if you press on the corner, the top will open and expose me to your sight in a state of nature. It is not possible, dearest, that a woman can ever have loved you as I do. Our friend excites my passion by the flattering opinion that he entertains of you. I cannot decide whether I am more fortunate in my friend or in my lover, for I could not imagine any being superior to either one or the other."

The case contained a gold snuff-box, and a small quantity of Spanish snuff which had been left in it proved that it had been used. I followed the instructions given in the letter, and I first saw my mistress in the costume of a nun, standing and in half profile. The second secret spring brought her before my eyes, entirely naked, lying on a mattress of black satin, in the position of the Madeleine of Coreggio. She was looking at Love, who had the quiver at his feet, and was gracefully sitting on the nun's robes. It was such a beautiful present that I did not think myself worthy of it. I wrote to M—— M—— a letter in which the deepest gratitude was blended with the most exalted love. The drawers of the bureau contained all her diamonds and four purses full of sequins. I admired her noble confidence in me. I locked the bureau, leaving everything undisturbed, and returned to Venice. If I had been able to escape out of the capricious clutches of fortune by giving up gambling, my happiness would have been complete.

My own portrait was set with rare perfection, and as it was arranged to be worn round the neck I attached it to six yards of Venetian chain, which made it a very handsome present. The secret was in the ring to which it was suspended, and it was very difficult to discover it. To make the spring work and expose my likeness it was necessary to pull the ring with some force and in a peculiar manner. Otherwise, nothing could be seen but the Annunciation; and it was then a beautiful ornament for a nun.

On Twelfth Night, having the locket and chain in my pocket, I went early in the evening to watch near the fine statue erected to the hero Colleoni after he had been poisoned, if history does not deceive us. 'Sit divus, modo non vivus', is a sentence from the enlightened monarch, which will last as long as there are monarchs on earth.

At six o'clock precisely my mistress alighted from the gondola, well dressed and well masked, but this time in the garb of a woman. We went to the Saint Samuel opera, and after the second ballet we repaired to the 'ridotto', where she amused herself by looking at all the ladies of the nobility who alone had the right to walk about without masks. After rambling about for half an hour, we entered the hall where the bank was held. She stopped before the table of M. Mocenigo, who at that time was the best amongst all the noble gamblers. As nobody was playing, he was carelessly whispering to a masked lady, whom I recognized as Madame Marina Pitani, whose adorer he was.

M—— M—— enquired whether I wanted to play, and as I answered in the negative she said to me,

"I take you for my partner."

And without waiting for my answer she took a purse, and placed a pile of gold on a card. The banker without disturbing himself shuffled the cards, turned them up, and my friend won the paroli. The banker paid, took another pack of cards, and continued his conversation with his lady, shewing complete indifference for four hundred sequins which my friend had already placed on the same card. The banker continuing his conversations, M—— M—— said to me, in excellent French,

"Our stakes are not high enough to interest this gentleman; let us go."

I took up the gold, which I put in my pocket, without answering M. de

Mocenigo, who said to me:

"Your mask is too exacting."

I rejoined my lovely gambler, who was surrounded. We stopped soon afterwards before the bank of M. Pierre Marcello, a charming young man, who had near him Madame Venier, sister of the patrician Momolo. My mistress began to play, and lost five rouleaux of gold one after the other. Having no more money, she took handfuls of gold from my pocket, and in four or five deals she broke the bank. She went away, and the noble banker, bowing, complimented her upon her good fortune. After I had taken care of all the gold she had won, I gave her my arm, and we left the 'ridotto', but remarking that a few inquisitive persons were following us, I took a gondola which landed us according to my instructions. One can always escape prying eyes in this way in Venice.

After supper I counted our winnings, and I found myself in possession of one thousand sequins as my share. I rolled the remainder in paper, and my friend asked me to put it in her bureau. I then took my locket and threw it over her neck; it gave her the greatest delight, and she tried for a long time to discover the secret. At last I showed it her, and she pronounced my portrait an excellent likeness.

Recollecting that we had but three hours to devote to the pleasures of love, I entreated her to allow me to turn them to good account.

"Yes," she said, "but be prudent, for our friend pretends that you might die on the spot."

"And why does he not fear the same danger for you, when your ecstasies are in reality much more frequent than mine?"

"He says that the liquor distilled by us women does not come from the brain, as is the case with men, and that the generating parts of woman have no contact with her intellect. The consequence of it, he says, is that the child is not the offspring of the mother as far as the brain, the seat of reason, is concerned, but of the father, and it seems to me very true. In that important act the woman has scarcely the amount of reason that she is in need of, and she cannot have any left to enable her to give a dose to the being she is generating."

"Your friend is a very learned man. But do you know that such a way of arguing opens my eyes singularly? It is evident that, if that system be true, women ought to be forgiven for all the follies which they commit on account of love, whilst man is inexcusable, and I should be in despair if I happened to place you in a position to become a mother."

"I shall know before long, and if it should be the case so much the better. My mind is made up, and my decision taken."

"And what is that decision?"

"To abandon my destiny entirely to you both. I am quite certain that neither one nor the other would let me remain at the convent."

"It would be a fatal event which would decide our future destinies. I would carry you off, and take you to England to marry you."

"My friend thinks that a physician might be bought, who, under the pretext of some disease of his own invention, would prescribe to me to go somewhere to drink the waters—a permission which the bishop might grant. At the watering-place I would get cured, and come back here, but I would much rather unite our destinies for ever. Tell me, dearest, could you manage to live anywhere as comfortably as you do here?"

"Alas! my love, no, but with you how could I be unhappy? But we will resume that subject whenever it may be necessary. Let us go to bed."

"Yes. If I have a son my friend wishes to act towards him as a father."

"Would he believe himself to be the father?"

"You might both of you believe it, but some likeness would soon enlighten me as to which of you two was the true father."

"Yes. If, for instance, the child composed poetry, then you would suppose that he was the son of your friend."

"How do you know that my friend can write poetry?"

"Admit that he is the author of the six lines which you wrote in answer to mine."

"I cannot possibly admit such a falsehood, because, good or bad, they were of my own making, and so as to leave you no doubt let me convince you of it at once."

"Oh, never mind! I believe you, and let us go to bed, or Love will call out the god of Parnassus."

"Let him do it, but take this pencil and write; I am Apollo, you may   be Love:"

Je ne me battrai pas; je te cede la place. Si Venus est ma soeur, L'Amour est de ma race. Je sais faire des vers. Un instant de perdu N'offense pas L'Amour, si je l'ai convaincu.

"It is on my knees that I entreat your pardon, my heavenly friend, but how could I expect so much talent in a young daughter of Venice, only twenty-two years of age, and, above all, brought up in a convent?"

"I have a most insatiate desire to prove myself more and more worthy of you. Did you think I was prudent at the gaming-table?"

"Prudent enough to make the most intrepid banker tremble."

"I do not always play so well, but I had taken you as a partner, and I felt I could set fortune at defiance. Why would you not play?"

"Because I had lost four thousand sequins last week and I was without money, but I shall play to-morrow, and fortune will smile upon me. In the mean time, here is a small book which I have brought from your boudoir: the postures of Pietro Aretino; I want to try some of them."

"The thought is worthy of you, but some of these positions could not be executed, and others are insipid."

"True, but I have chosen four very interesting ones."

These delightful labours occupied the remainder of the night until the alarum warned us that it was time to part. I accompanied my lovely nun as far as her gondola, and then went to bed; but I could not sleep. I got up in order to go and pay a few small debts, for one of the greatest pleasures that a spendthrift can enjoy is, in my opinion, to discharge certain liabilities. The gold won by my mistress proved lucky for me, for I did not pass a single day of the carnival without winning.

Three days after Twelfth Night, having paid a visit to the casino of Muran for the purpose of placing some gold in M—— M—— 's bureau, the door-keeper handed me a letter from my nun. Laura had, a few minutes before, delivered me one from C—— C——.

My new mistress, after giving me an account of her health, requested me to enquire from my jeweller whether he had not by chance made a ring having on its bezel a St. Catherine which, without a doubt, concealed another portrait; she wished to know the secret of that ring. "A young boarder," she added, "a lovely girl, and my friend, is the owner of that ring. There must be a secret, but she does not know it." I answered that I would do what she wished. But here is the letter of C—— C——. It was rather amusing, because it placed me in a regular dilemma; it bore a late date, but the letter of M—— M—— had been written two days before it.

"Ali! how truly happy I am, my beloved husband! You love Sister M—— M——, my dear friend. She has a locket as big as a ring, and she cannot have received it from anyone but you. I am certain that your dear likeness is to be found under the Annunciation. I recognized the style of the artist, and it is certainly the same who painted the locket and my ring. I am satisfied that Sister M—-M—-has received that present from you. I am so pleased to know all that I would not run the risk of grieving her by telling her that I knew her secret, but my dear friend, either more open or more curious, has not imitated my reserve. She told me that she had no doubt of my St. Catherine concealing the portrait of my lover. Unable to say anything better, I told her that the ring was in reality a gift from my lover, but that I had no idea of his portrait being concealed inside of it. 'If it is as you say,' observed M—— M——, 'and if you have no objection, I will try to find out the secret, and afterwards I will let you know mine.' Being quite certain that she would not discover it, I gave her my ring, saying that, if she could find out the secret, I should be very much pleased.

"Just as that moment my aunt paid me a visit, and I left my ring in the hands of M—— M——, who returned it to me after dinner, assuring me that, although she had not been able to find out the secret, she was certain there was one. I promise you that she shall never hear anything about it from me, because if she saw your portrait, she would guess everything, and then I should have to tell her who you are. I am sorry to be compelled to conceal anything from her, but I am very glad you love one another. I pity you both, however, with all my heart, because I know that you are obliged to make love through a grating in that horrid parlour. How I wish, dearest, I could give you my place! I would make two persons happy at the same time! Adieu!"

I answered that she had guessed rightly, that the locket of her friend was a present from me and contained my likeness, but that she was to keep the secret, and to be certain that my friendship for M—— M—— interfered in no way with the feeling which bound me to her for ever. I certainly was well aware that I was not behaving in a straightforward manner, but I endeavoured to deceive myself, so true it is that a woman, weak as she is, has more influence by the feeling she inspires than man can possibly have with all his strength. At all events, I was foolishly trying to keep up an intrigue which I knew to be near its denouement through the intimacy that had sprung up between these two friendly rivals.

Laura having informed me that there was to be on a certain day a ball in the large parlour of the convent, I made up my mind to attend it in such a disguise that my two friends could not recognize me. I decided upon the costume of a Pierrot, because it conceals the form and the gait better than any other. I was certain that my two friends would be behind the grating, and that it would afford me the pleasant opportunity of seeing them together and of comparing them. In Venice, during the carnival, that innocent pleasure is allowed in convents. The guests dance in the parlour, and the sisters remain behind the grating, enjoying the sight of the ball, which is over by sunset. Then all the guests retire, and the poor nuns are for a long time happy in the recollection of the pleasure enjoyed by their eyes. The ball was to take place in the afternoon of the day appointed for my meeting with M—— M——, in the evening at the casino of Muran, but that could not prevent me from going to the ball; besides, I wanted to see my dear C—— C——.

I have said before that the dress of a Pierrot is the costume which disguises the figure and the gait most completely. It has also the advantage, through a large cap, of concealing the hair, and the white gauze which covers the face does not allow the colour of the eyes or of the eyebrows to be seen, but in order to prevent the costume from hindering the movements of the mask, he must not wear anything underneath, and in winter a dress made of light calico is not particularly agreeable. I did not, however, pay any attention to that, and taking only a plate of soup I went to Muran in a gondola. I had no cloak, and—in my pockets I had nothing but my handkerchief, my purse, and the key of the casino.

I went at once to the convent. The parlour was full, but thanks to my costume of Pierrot, which was seen in Venice but very seldom, everybody made room for me. I walked on, assuming the gait of a booby, the true characteristic of my costume, and I stopped near the dancers. After I had examined the Pantaloons, Punches, Harlequins, and Merry Andrews, I went near the grating, where I saw all the nuns and boarders, some seated, some standing, and, without appearing to, notice any of them in particular, I remarked my two friends together, and very intent upon the dancers. I then walked round the room, eyeing everybody from head to foot, and calling the general attention upon myself.

I chose for my partner in the minuet a pretty girl dressed as a Columbine, and I took her hand in so awkward a manner and with such an air of stupidity that everybody laughed and made room for us. My partner danced very well according to her costume, and I kept my character with such perfection that the laughter was general. After the minuet I danced twelve forlanas with the greatest vigour. Out of breath, I threw myself on a sofa, pretending to go to sleep, and the moment I began to snore everybody respected the slumbers of Pierrot. The quadrille lasted one hour, and I took no part in it, but immediately after it, a Harlequin approached me with the impertinence which belongs to his costume, and flogged me with his wand. It is Harlequin's weapon. In my quality of Pierrot I had no weapons. I seized him round the waist and carried him round the parlour, running all the time, while he kept on flogging me. I then put him down. Adroitly snatching his wand out of his hand, I lifted his Columbine on my shoulders, and pursued him, striking him with the wand, to the great delight and mirth of the company. The Columbine was screaming because she was afraid of my tumbling down and of shewing her centre of gravity to everybody in the fall. She had good reason to fear, for suddenly a foolish Merry Andrew came behind me, tripped me up, and down I tumbled. Everybody hooted Master Punch. I quickly picked myself up, and rather vexed I began a regular fight with the insolent fellow. He was of my size, but awkward, and he had nothing but strength. I threw him, and shaking him vigorously on all sides I contrived to deprive him of his hump and false stomach. The nuns, who had never seen such a merry sight, clapped their hands, everybody laughed loudly, and improving my opportunity I ran through the crowd and disappeared.

I was in a perspiration, and the weather was cold; I threw myself into a gondola, and in order not to get chilled I landed at the 'ridotto'. I had two hours to spare before going to the casino of Muran, and I longed to enjoy the astonishment of my beautiful nun when she saw M. Pierrot standing before her. I spent those two hours in playing at all the banks, winning, losing, and performing all sorts of antics with complete freedom, being satisfied that no one could recognize me; enjoying the present, bidding defiance to the future, and laughing at all those reasonable beings who exercise their reason to avoid the misfortunes which they fear, destroying at the same time the pleasure that they might enjoy.

But two o'clock struck and gave me warning that Love and Comus were calling me to bestow new delights upon me. With my pockets full of gold and silver, I left the ridotto, hurried to Muran, entered the sanctuary, and saw my divinity leaning against the mantelpiece. She wore her convent dress. I come near her by stealth, in order to enjoy her surprise. I look at her, and I remain petrified, astounded.

The person I see is not M—— M——

It is C—— C——, dressed as a nun, who, more astonished even than myself, does not utter one word or make a movement. I throw myself in an arm-chair in order to breathe and to recover from my surprise. The sight of C—— C—— had annihilated me, and my mind was as much stupefied as my body. I found myself in an inextricable maze.

It is M—— M——, I said to myself, who has played that trick upon me, but how has she contrived to know that I am the lover of C—— C——? Has C—— C—— betrayed my secret? But if she has betrayed it, how could M—— M—— deprive herself of the pleasure of seeing me, and consent to her place being taken by her friend and rival? That cannot be a mark of kind compliance, for a woman never carries it to such an extreme. I see in it only a mark of contempt—a gratuitous insult.

My self-love tried hard to imagine some reason likely to disprove the possibility of that contempt, but in vain. Absorbed in that dark discontent, I believed myself wantonly trifled with, deceived, despised, and I spent half an hour silent and gloomy, staring at C—— C——, who scarcely dared to breathe, perplexed, confused, and not knowing in whose presence she was, for she could only know me as the Pierrot whom she had seen at the ball.

Deeply in love with M—— M——, and having come to the casino only for her, I did not feel disposed to accept the exchange, although I was very far from despising C—— C——, whose charms were as great, at least, as those of M—— M——. I loved her tenderly, I adored her, but at that moment it was not her whom I wanted, because at first her presence had struck me as a mystification. It seemed to me that if I celebrated the return of C—— C—— in an amorous manner, I would fail in what I owed to myself, and I thought that I was bound in honour not to lend myself to the imposition. Besides, without exactly realizing that

feeling, I was not sorry to have it in my power to reproach M——
M—— with an indifference very strange in a woman in love, and
I wanted to act in such a manner that she should not be able to
say that she had procured me a pleasure. I must add that I
suspected M—— M—— to be hiding in the secret closet, perhaps
with her friend.

I had to take a decision, for I could not pass the whole night in my
costume of Pierrot, and without speaking. At first I thought of
going away, the more so that both C—— C—— and her friend
could not be certain that I and Pierrot were the same individual,
but I soon abandoned the idea with horror, thinking of the deep
sorrow which would fill the loving soul of C—— C—— if she ever
heard I was the Pierrot. I almost fancied that she knew it already,
and I shared the grief which she evidently would feel in that case. I
had seduced her. I had given her the right to call me her husband.
These thoughts broke my heart.

If M—— M—— is in the closet, said I to myself, she will shew
herself in good time. With that idea, I took off the gauze which
covered my features. My lovely C—— C—— gave a deep sigh, and
said:

"I breathe again! it could not be anyone but you, my heart felt it.
You seemed surprised when you saw me, dearest; did you not
know that I was waiting for you?"

"I had not the faintest idea of it."

"If you are angry, I regret it deeply, but I am innocent."

"My adored friend, come to my arms, and never suppose that I can be angry with you. I am delighted to see you; you are always my dear wife: but I entreat you to clear up a cruel doubt, for you could never have betrayed my secret."

"I! I would never have been guilty of such a thing, even if death had stared me in the face."

"Then, how did you come here? How did your friend contrive to discover everything? No one but you could tell her that I am your husband. Laura perhaps....'

"No, Laura is faithful, dearest, and I cannot guess how it was."

"But how could you be persuaded to assume that disguise, and to come here? You can leave the convent, and you have never apprised me of that important circumstance."

"Can you suppose that I would not have told you all about it, if I had ever left the convent, even once? I came out of it two hours ago, for the first time, and I was induced to take that step in the simplest, the most natural manner."

"Tell me all about it, my love. I feel extremely curious."

"I am glad of it, and I would conceal nothing from you. You know how dearly M—— M—— and I love each other. No intimacy could be more tender than ours; you can judge of it by what I told you in my letters. Well, two days ago, my dear friend begged the abbess and my aunt to allow me to sleep in her room in the place of the lay-sister, who, having a very bad cold, had carried her cough to the infirmary. The permission was granted, and you cannot imagine our pleasure in seeing ourselves at liberty, for the first time, to sleep in the same bed. To-day, shortly after you had left the parlour, where you so much amused us, without our discovering that the delightful Pierrot was our friend, my dear M—— M—— retired to her room and I followed her. The moment we were alone she told me that she wanted me to render her a service from which depended our happiness. I need not tell you how readily I answered that she had only to name it. Then she opened a drawer, and much to my surprise she dressed me in this costume. She was laughing; and I did the same without suspecting the end of the joke. When she saw me entirely metamorphosed into a nun, she told me that she was going to trust me with a great secret, but that she entertained no fear of my discretion. 'Let me tell you, clearest friend,' she said to me, 'that I was on the point of going out of the convent, to return only tomorrow morning. I have, however, just decided that you shall go instead. You have nothing to fear and you do not require any instructions, because I know that you will meet with no difficulty. In an hour, a lay-sister will come here, I will speak a few words apart to her, and she will tell you to follow her. You will go out with her through the small gate and across the garden as far as the room leading out to the low shore. There you will get into the gondola, and say to the gondolier these words: 'To the casino.' You will reach it in five minutes; you will step out and enter a small apartment, where you will find a good fire; you will be alone, and you will wait.' 'For whom? I enquired. 'For nobody. You need not know any more: you may only be certain that nothing unpleasant will happen to you; trust me for that. You will sup at the casino, and sleep, if you like, without being disturbed. Do not ask any questions, for I cannot answer them. Such is, my dear husband, the whole truth. Tell me now what I could do after that speech of my friend, and after she had received my promise to do whatever she wished. Do not distrust what I tell you, for my lips cannot utter a falsehood. I laughed, and not expecting anything else but an agreeable adventure, I followed the lay-sister and soon found myself here. After a tedious hour of expectation, Pierrot made his appearance. Be quite certain that the very moment I saw you my heart knew who it was, but a minute after I felt as if the lightning had struck me when I saw you step back, for I saw clearly enough that you did not expect to find me. Your gloomy silence frightened me, and I would never have dared to be the first in breaking it; the more so that, in spite of the feelings of my heart, I might have been mistaken. The dress of Pierrot might conceal some other man, but certainly no one that I could have seen in this place without horror. Recollect that for the last eight months I have been deprived of the happiness of kissing you, and now that you must be certain of my innocence, allow me to congratulate you upon knowing this casino. You are happy, and I congratulate you with all my heart. M—— M—— is, after me, the only woman worthy of your love, the only one with whom I could consent to share it. I used to pity you, but I do so no longer, and your happiness makes me happy. Kiss me now."

I should have been very ungrateful, I should, even have been cruel, if I had not then folded in my arms with the warmth of true love the angel of goodness and beauty who was before me, thanks to the most wonderful effort of friendship.

After assuring her that I no longer entertained any doubt of her innocence, I told her that I thought the behaviour of her friend very ambiguous. I said that, notwithstanding the pleasure I felt in seeing her, the trick played upon me by her friend was a very bad one, that it could not do otherwise than displease me greatly, because it was an insult to me.

"I am not of your opinion," replied C—— C——.

"My dear M—— M—— has evidently contrived, somehow or other, to discover that, before you were acquainted with her, you were my lover. She thought very likely that you still loved me, and she imagined, for I know her well, that she could not give us a greater proof of her love than by procuring us, without forewarning us, that which two lovers fond of each other must wish for so ardently. She wished to make us happy, and I cannot be angry with her for it."

"You are right to think so, dearest, but my position is very different from yours. You have not another lover; you could not have another; but I being free and unable to see you, have not found it possible to resist the charms of M—— M——. I love her madly; she knows it, and, intelligent as she is, she must have meant to shew her contempt for me by doing what she has done. I candidly confess that I feel hurt in the highest degree. If she loved me as I love her, she never could have sent you here instead of coming herself."

"I do not think so, my beloved friend. Her soul is as noble as her heart is generous; and just in the same manner that I am not sorry to know that you love one another and that you make each other happy, as this beautiful casino proves to me, she does not regret our love, and she is, on the contrary, delighted to shew us that she approves of it. Most likely she meant to prove that she loved you for your own sake, that your happiness makes her happy, and that she is not jealous of her best friend being her rival. To convince you that you ought not to be angry with her for having discovered our secret, she proves, by sending me here in her place, that she is pleased to see your heart divided between her and me. You know very well that she loves me, and that I am often either her wife or her husband, and as you do not object to my being your rival and making her often as happy as I can, she does not want you either to suppose that her love is like hatred, for the love of a jealous heart is very much like it."

"You plead the cause of your friend with the eloquence of an angel, but, dear little wife, you do not see the affair in its proper light. You have intelligence and a pure soul, but you have not my experience. M—— M——'s love for me has been nothing but a passing fancy, and she knows that I am not such an idiot as to be deceived by all this affair. I am miserable, and it is her doing."

"Then I should be right if I complained of her also, because she makes me feel that she is the mistress of my lover, and she shews me that, after seducing him from me, she gives him back to me without difficulty. Then she wishes me to understand that she despises also my tender affection for her, since she places me in a position to shew that affection for another person."

"Now, dearest, you speak without reason, for the relations between you two are of an entirely different nature. Your mutual love is nothing but trifling nonsense, mere illusion of the senses. The pleasures which you enjoy together are not exclusive. To become jealous of one another it would be necessary that one of you two should feel a similar affection for another woman but M—— M—— could no more be angry at your having a lover than you could be so yourself if she had one; provided, however, that the lover should not belong to the other."

"But that is precisely our case, and you are mistaken. We are not angry at your loving us both equally. Have I not written to you that I would most willingly give you my place near M—— M——? Then you must believe that I despise you likewise?"

"My darling, that wish of yours to give me up your place, when you did not know that I was happy with M—— M——, arose from your friendship rather than from your love, and for the present I must be glad to see that your friendship is stronger than your love, but I have every reason to be sorry when M—— M—— feels the same. I love her without any possibility of marrying her. Do you understand me, dearest? As for you, knowing that you must be my wife, I am certain of our love, which practice will animate with new life. It is not the same with M—— M——; that love cannot spring up again into existence. Is it not humiliating for me to have inspired her with nothing but a passing fancy? I understand your adoration for her very well. She has initiated you into all her mysteries, and you owe her eternal friendship and everlasting gratitude."

It was midnight, and we went on wasting our time in this desultory conversation, when the prudent and careful servant brought us an excellent supper. I could not touch anything, my heart was too full, but my dear little wife supped with a good appetite. I could not help laughing when I saw a salad of whites of eggs, and C—— C—— thought it extraordinary because all the yolks had been removed. In her innocence, she could not understand the intention of the person who had ordered the supper. As I looked at her, I was compelled to acknowledge that she had improved in beauty; in fact C—— C—— was remarkably beautiful, yet I remained cold by her side. I have always thought that there is no merit in being faithful to the person we truly love.

Two hours before day-light we resumed our seats near the fire, and C—— C——, seeing how dull I was, was delicately attentive to me. She attempted no allurement, all her movements wore the stamp of the most decent reserve, and her conversation, tender in its expressions and perfectly easy, never conveyed the shadow of a reproach for my coolness.

Towards the end of our long conversation, she asked me what she should say to her friend on her return to the convent.

"My dear M—— M—— expects to see me full of joy and gratitude for the generous present she thought she was making me by giving me this night, but what shall I tell her?"

"The whole truth. Do not keep from her a single word of our conversation, as far as your memory will serve you, and tell her especially that she has made me miserable for a long time."

"No, for I should cause her too great a sorrow; she loves you dearly, and cherishes the locket which contains your likeness. I mean, on the contrary, to do all I can to bring peace between you two, and I must succeed before long, because my friend is not guilty of any wrong, and you only feel some spite, although with no cause. I will send you my letter by Laura, unless you promise me to go and fetch it yourself at her house."

"Your letters will always be dear to me, but, mark my words, M—— M—— will not enter into any explanation. She will believe you in everything, except in one."

"I suppose you mean our passing a whole night together as innocently as if we were brother and sister. If she knows you as well as I do, she will indeed think it most wonderful."

"In that case, you may tell her the contrary, if you like."

"Nothing of the sort. I hate falsehoods, and I will certainly never utter one in such a case as this; it would be very wrong. I do not love you less on that account, my darling, although, during this long night, you have not condescended to give me the slightest proof of your love."

"Believe me, dearest, I am sick from unhappiness. I love you with my whole soul, but I am in such a situation that...."

"What! you are weeping, my love! Oh! I entreat you, spare my heart! I am so sorry to have told you such a thing, but I can assure you I never meant to make you unhappy. I am sure that in a quarter of an hour M—— M—— will be crying likewise."

The alarum struck, and, having no longer any hope of seeing M—— M—— come to justify herself, I kissed C—— C——. I gave her the key of the casino, requesting her to return it for me to M—— M——, and my young friend having gone back to the convent, I put on my mask and left the casino.

CHAPTER XX

I Am in Danger of Perishing in the Lagunes—Illness—Letters from C. C. and M. M.—The Quarrel is Made Up—Meeting at the Casino of Muran I Learn the Name of M. M.'s Friend, and Consent to Give Him A Supper at My Casino in the Company of Our Common Mistress

The weather was fearful. The wind was blowing fiercely, and it was bitterly cold. When I reached the shore, I looked for a gondola, I called the gondoliers, but, in contravention to the police regulations, there was neither gondola nor gondolier. What was I to do? Dressed in light linen, I was hardly in a fit state to walk along the wharf for an hour in such weather. I should most likely have gone back to the casino if I had had the key, but I was paying the penalty of the foolish spite which had made me give it up. The wind almost carried me off my feet, and there was no house that I could enter to get a shelter.

I had in my pockets three hundred philippes that I had won in the evening, and a purse full of gold. I had therefore every reason to fear the thieves of Muran—a very dangerous class of cutthroats, determined murderers who enjoyed and abused a certain impunity, because they had some privileges granted to them by the Government on account of the services they rendered in the manufactories of looking-glasses and in the glassworks which are numerous on the island. In order to prevent their emigration, the Government had granted them the freedom of Venice. I dreaded meeting a pair of them, who would have stripped me of everything, at least. I had not, by chance, with me the knife which all honest men must carry to defend their lives in my dear country. I was truly in an unpleasant predicament.

I was thus painfully situated when I thought I could see a light through the crevices of a small house. I knocked modestly against the shutter. A voice called out:

"Who is knocking?"

And at the same moment the shutter was pushed open.

"What do you want?" asked a man, rather astonished at my costume.

I explained my predicament in a few words, and giving him one sequin I begged his permission to shelter myself under his roof. Convinced by my sequin rather than my words, he opened the door, I went in, and promising him another sequin for his trouble I requested him to get me a gondola to take me to Venice. He dressed himself hurriedly, thanking God for that piece of good fortune, and went out assuring me that he would soon get me a gondola. I remained alone in a miserable room in which all his family, sleeping together in a large, ill-looking bed, were staring at me in consequence of my extraordinary costume. In half an hour the good man returned to announce that the gondoliers were at the wharf, but that they wanted to be paid in advance. I raised no objection, gave a sequin to the man for his trouble, and went to the wharf.

The sight of two strong gondoliers made me get into the gondola without anxiety, and we left the shore without being much disturbed by the wind, but when we had gone beyond the island, the storm attacked us with such fury that I thought myself lost, for, although a good swimmer, I was not sure I had strength enough to resist the violence of the waves and swim to the shore. I ordered the men to go back to the island, but they answered that I had not to deal with a couple of cowards, and that I had no occasion to be afraid. I knew the disposition of our gondoliers, and I made up my mind to say no more.

But the wind increased in violence, the foaming waves rushed into the gondola, and my two rowers, in spite of their vigour and of their courage, could no longer guide it. We were only within one hundred yards of the mouth of the Jesuits' Canal, when a terrible gust of wind threw one of the 'barcarols' into the sea; most fortunately he contrived to hold by the gondola and to get in again, but he had lost his oar, and while he was securing another the gondola had tacked, and had already gone a considerable distance abreast. The position called for immediate decision, and I had no wish to take my supper with Neptune. I threw a handful of philippes into the gondola, and ordered the gondoliers to throw overboard the 'felce' which covered the boat. The ringing of money, as much as the imminent danger, ensured instant obedience, and then, the wind having less hold upon us, my brave boatmen shewed AEolus that their efforts could conquer him, for in less than five minutes we shot into the Beggars' Canal, and I reached the Bragadin Palace. I went to bed at once, covering myself heavily in order to regain my natural heat, but sleep, which alone could have restored me to health, would not visit me.

Five or six hours afterwards, M. de Bragadin and his two inseparable friends paid me a visit, and found me raving with fever. That did not prevent my respectable protector from laughing at the sight of the costume of Pierrot lying on the sofa. After congratulating me upon having escaped with my life out of such a bad predicament, they left me alone. In the evening I perspired so profusely that my bed had to be changed. The next day my fever and delirium increased, and two days after, the fever having abated, I found myself almost crippled and suffering fearfully with lumbago. I felt that nothing could relieve me but a strict regimen, and I bore the evil patiently.

Early on the Wednesday morning, Laura, the faithful messenger, called on me; I was still in my bed: I told her that I could neither read nor write, and I asked her to come again the next day. She placed on the table, near my bed, the parcel she had for me, and she left me, knowing what had occurred to me sufficiently to enable her to inform C—— C—— of the state in which I was.

Feeling a little better towards the evening, I ordered my servant to lock me in my room, and I opened C—— C——'s letter. The first thing I found in the parcel, and which caused me great pleasure, was the key of the casino which she returned to me. I had already repented having given it up, and I was beginning to feel that I had been in the wrong. It acted like a refreshing balm upon me. The second thing, not less dear after the return of the precious key, was a letter from M—— M——, the seal of which I was not long in breaking, and I read the following lines:

"The particulars which you have read, or which you are going to read, in the letter of my friend, will cause you, I hope, to forget the fault which I have committed so innocently, for I trusted, on the contrary, that you would be very happy. I saw all and heard all, and you would not have gone away without the key if I had not, most unfortunately, fallen asleep an hour before your departure. Take back the key and come to the casino to-morrow night, since Heaven has saved you from the storm. Your love may, perhaps, give you the right to complain, but not to ill-treat a woman who certainly has not given you any mark of contempt."

I afterwards read the letter of my dear C—— C——, and I will give a copy of it here, because I think it will prove interesting:

"I entreat you, dear husband, not to send back this key, unless you have become the most cruel of men, unless you find pleasure in tormenting two women who, love you ardently, and who love you for yourself only. Knowing your excellent heart, I trust you will go to the casino to-morrow evening and make it up with M—— M——, who cannot go there to-night. You will see that you are in the wrong, dearest, and that, far from despising you, my dear friend loves you only. In the mean time, let me tell you what you are not acquainted with, and what you must be anxious to know.

"Immediately after you had gone away in that fearful storm which caused me such anguish, and just as I was preparing to return to the convent, I was much surprised to see standing before me my dear M—— M——, who from some hiding-place had heard all you had said. She had several times been on the point of shewing herself, but she had always been prevented by the fear of coming out of season, and thus stopping a reconciliation which she thought was inevitable between two fond lovers. Unfortunately, sleep had conquered her before your departure, and she only woke when the alarum struck, too late to detain you, for you had rushed with the haste of a man who is flying from some terrible danger. As soon as I saw her, I gave her the key, although I did not know what it meant, and my friend, heaving a deep sigh, told me that she would explain everything as soon as we were safe in her room. We left the casino in a dreadful storm, trembling for your safety, and not thinking of our own danger. As soon as we were in the convent I resumed my usual costume, and M—— M—— went to bed. I took a seat near her, and this is what she told me. 'When you left your ring in my hands to go to your aunt, who had sent for you, I examined it with so much attention that at last I suspected the small blue spot to be connected with the secret spring; I took a pin, succeeded in removing the top part, and I cannot express the joy I felt when I saw that we both loved the same man, but no more can I give you an idea of my sorrow when I thought that I was encroaching upon your rights. Delighted, however, with my discovery, I immediately conceived a plan which would procure you the pleasure of supping with him. I closed the ring again and returned it to you, telling you at the same time that I had not been able to discover anything. I was then truly the happiest of women. Knowing your heart, knowing that you were aware of the love of your lover for me, since I had innocently shewed you his portrait, and happy in the idea that you were not jealous of me, I would have despised myself if I had entertained any feelings different from your own, the more so that your rights over him were by far stronger than mine. As for the mysterious manner in which you always kept from me the name of your husband, I easily guessed that you were only obeying his orders, and I admired your noble sentiments and the goodness of your heart. In my opinion your lover was afraid of losing us both, if we found out that neither the one nor the other of us possessed his whole heart. I could not express my deep sorrow when I thought that, after you had seen me in possession of his portrait, you continued to act in the same manner towards me, although you could not any longer hope to be the sole object of his love. Then I had but one idea; to prove to both of you that M—— M—— is worthy of your affection, of your friendship, of your esteem. I was indeed thoroughly happy when I thought that the felicity of our trio would be increased a hundredfold, for is it not an unbearable misery to keep a secret from the being we adore? I made you take my place, and I thought that proceeding a masterpiece. You allowed me to dress you as a nun, and with a compliance which proves your confidence in me you went to my casino without knowing where you were going. As soon as you had landed, the gondola came back, and I went to a place well known to our friend from which, without being seen, I could follow all your movements and hear everything you said. I was the author of the play; it was natural that I should witness it, the more so that I felt certain of seeing and hearing nothing that would not be very agreeable to me. I reached the casino a quarter of an hour after you, and I cannot tell you my delightful surprise when I saw that dear Pierrot who had amused us so much, and whom we had not recognized. But I was fated to feel no other pleasure than that of his appearance. Fear, surprise, and anxiety overwhelmed me at once when I saw the effect produced upon him by the disappointment of his expectation, and I felt unhappy. Our lover took the thing wrongly, and he went away in despair; he loves me still, but if he thinks of me it is only to try to forget me. Alas! he will succeed but too soon! By sending back that key he proves that he will never again go to the casino. Fatal night! When my only wish was to minister to the happiness of three persons, how is it that the very reverse of my wish has occurred? It will kill me, dear friend, unless you contrive to make him understand reason, for I feel that without him I cannot live. You must have the means of writing to him, you know him, you know his name. In the name of all goodness, send back this key to him with a letter to persuade him to come to the casino to-morrow or on the following day, if it is only to speak to me; and I hope to convince him of my love and my innocence. Rest to-day, dearest, but to-morrow write to him, tell him the whole truth; take pity on your poor friend, and forgive her for loving your lover. I shall write a few lines myself; you will enclose them in your letter. It is my fault if he no longer loves you; you ought to hate me, and yet you are generous enough to love me. I adore you; I have seen his tears, I have seen how well his soul can love; I know him now. I could not have believed that men were able to love so much. I have passed a terrible night. Do not think I am angry, dear friend, because you confided to him that we love one another like two lovers; it does not displease me, and with him it was no indiscretion, because his mind is as free of prejudices as his heart is good.'

"Tears were choking her. I tried to console her, and I most willingly promised her to write to you. She never closed her eyes throughout that day, but I slept soundly for four hours.

"When we got up we found the convent full of bad news, which interested us a great deal more than people imagined. It was reported that, an hour before daybreak, a fishing-boat had been lost in the lagune, that two gondolas had been capsized, and that the people in them had perished. You may imagine our anguish! We dared not ask any questions, but it was just the hour at which you had left me, and we entertained the darkest forebodings. We returned to our room, where M—— M—— fainted away. More courageous than she is, I told her that you were a good swimmer, but I could not allay her anxiety, and she went to bed with a feverish chill. Just at that moment, my aunt, who is of a very cheerful disposition, came in, laughing, to tell us that during the storm the Pierrot who had made us laugh so much had had a narrow escape of being drowned. 'Ah! the poor Pierrot!' I exclaimed, 'tell us all about him, dear aunt. I am very glad he was saved. Who is he? Do you know?' 'Oh! yes,' she answered, 'everything is known, for he was taken home by our gondoliers. One of them has just told me that Pierrot, having spent the night at the Briati ball, did not find any gondola to return to Venice, and that our gondoliers took him for a sequin. One of the men fell into the sea, but then the brave Pierrot, throwing handfuls of silver upon the 'Zenia' pitched the 'felce' over board, and the wind having less hold they reached Venice safely through the Beggars' Canal. This morning the lucky gondoliers divided thirty philippes which they found in the gondola, and they have been fortunate enough to pick up their 'felce'. Pierrot will remember Muran and the ball at Briati. The man says that he is the son of M. de Bragadin, the procurator's brother. He was taken to the palace of that nobleman nearly dead from cold, for he was dressed in light calico, and had no cloak.'

"When my aunt had left us, we looked at one another for several minutes without uttering a word, but we felt that the good news had brought back life to us. M—— M—— asked me whether you were really the son of M, de Bragadin. 'It might be so,' I said to her, 'but his name does not shew my lover to be the bastard of that nobleman, and still less his legitimate child, for M. de Bragadin was never married.' 'I should be very sorry,' said M—— M——, 'if he were his son.' I thought it right, then, to tell her your true name, and of the application made to my father by M. de Bragadin for my hand, the consequence of which was that I had been shut up in the convent. Therefore, my own darling, your little wife has no longer any secret to keep from M—— M——, and I hope you will not accuse me of indiscretion, for it is better that our dear friend should know all the truth than only half of it. We have been greatly amused, as you may well suppose, by the certainty with which people say that you spent all the night at the Briati ball. When people do not know everything, they invent, and what might be is often accepted in the place of what is in reality; sometimes it proves very fortunate. At all events the news did a great deal of good to my friend, who is now much better. She has had an excellent night, and the hope of seeing you at the casino has restored all her beauty. She has read this letter three or four times, and has smothered me with kisses. I long to give her the letter which you are going to write to her. The messenger will wait for it. Perhaps I shall see you again at the casino, and in a better temper, I hope. Adieu."

It did not require much argument to conquer me. When I had finished the letter, I was at once the admirer of C—— C—— and the ardent lover of M—— M——. But, alas! although the fever had left me, I was crippled. Certain that Laura would come again early the next morning, I could not refrain from writing to both of them a short letter, it is true, but long enough to assure them that reason had again taken possession of my poor brain. I wrote to C—— C—— that she had done right in telling her friend my name, the more so that, as I did not attend their church any longer, I had no reason to make a mystery of it. In everything else I freely acknowledged myself in the wrong, and I promised her that I would atone by giving M—-M—— the strongest possible proofs of my repentance as soon as I could go again to her casino.

This is the letter that I wrote to my adorable nun:

"I gave C—— C—— the key of your casino, to be returned to you, my own charming friend, because I believed myself trifled with and despised, of malice aforethought, by the woman I worship. In my error I thought myself unworthy of presenting myself before your eyes, and, in spite of love, horror made me shudder. Such was the effect produced upon me by an act which would have appeared to me admirable, if my self-love had not blinded me and upset my reason. But, dearest, to admire it it would have been necessary for my mind to be as noble as yours, and I have proved how far it is from being so. I am inferior to you in all things, except in passionate love, and I will prove it to you at our next meeting, when I will beg on my knees a generous pardon. Believe me, beloved creature, if I wish ardently to recover my health, it is only to have it in my power to prove by my love a thousand times increased, how ashamed I am of my errors. My painful lumbago has alone prevented me from answering your short note yesterday, to express to you my regrets, and the love which has been enhanced in me by your generosity, alas! so badly rewarded. I can assure you that in the lagunes, with death staring me in the face, I regretted no one but you, nothing but having outraged you. But in the fearful danger then threatening me I only saw a punishment from Heaven. If I had not cruelly sent back to you the key of the casino, I should most likely have returned there, and should have avoided the sorrow as well as the physical pains which I am now suffering as an expiation. I thank you a thousand times for having recalled me to myself, and you may be certain that for the future I will keep better control over myself; nothing shall make me doubt your love. But, darling, what do you say of C—— C——? Is she not an incarnate angel who can be compared to no one but you? You love us both equally. I am the only one weak and faulty, and you make me ashamed of myself. Yet I feel that I would give my life for her as well as for you. I feel curious about one thing, but I cannot trust it to paper. You will satisfy that curiosity the first time I shall be able to go to the casino before two days at the earliest. I will let you know two days beforehand. In the mean time, I entreat you to think a little of me, and to be certain of my devoted love. Adieu."

The next morning Laura found me sitting up in bed, and in a fair way to recover my health. I requested her to tell C—— C—— that I felt much better, and I gave her the letter I had written. She had brought me one from my dear little wife, in which I found enclosed a note from M—— M——. Those two letter were full of tender expressions of love, anxiety for my health, and ardent prayers for my recovery.

Six days afterwards, feeling much stronger, I went to Muran, where the keeper of the casino handed me a letter from M—— M——. She wrote to me how impatient she was for my complete recovery, and how desirous she was to see me in possession of her casino, with all the privileges which she hoped I would retain for ever.

"Let me know, I entreat you," she added, "when we are likely to meet again, either at Muran or in Venice, as you please. Be quite certain that whenever we meet we shall be alone and without a witness."

I answered at once, telling her that we would meet the day after the morrow at her casino, because I wanted to receive her loving absolution in the very spot where I had outraged the most generous of women.

I was longing to see her again, for I was ashamed of my cruel injustice towards her, and panting to atone for my wrongs. Knowing her disposition, and reflecting calmly upon what had taken place, it was now evident to me that what she had done, very far from being a mark of contempt, was the refined effort of a love wholly devoted to me. Since she had found out that I was the lover of her young friend, could she imagine that my heart belonged only to herself? In the same way that her love for me did not prevent her from being compliant with the ambassador, she admitted the possibility of my being the same with C—— C——.

She overlooked the difference of constitution between the two sexes, and the privileges enjoyed by women.

Now that age has whitened my hair and deadened the ardour of my senses, my imagination does not take such a high flight, and I think differently. I am conscious that my beautiful nun sinned against womanly reserve and modesty, the two most beautiful appanages of the fair sex, but if that unique, or at least rare, woman was guilty of an eccentricity which I then thought a virtue, she was at all events exempt from that fearful venom called jealousy—an unhappy passion which devours the miserable being who is labouring under it, and destroys the love that gave it birth.

Two days afterwards, on the 4th of February, 1754, I had the supreme felicity of finding myself again alone with my beloved mistress. She wore the dress of a nun. As we both felt guilty, the moment we saw each other, by a spontaneous movement, we fell both on our knees, folded in each other's arms. We had both ill-treated Love; she had treated him like a child, I had adored him after the fashion of a Jansenist. But where could we have found the proper language for the excuses we had to address to each other for the mutual forgiveness we had to entreat and to grant? Kisses—that mute, yet expressive language, that delicate, voluptuous contact which sends sentiment coursing rapidly through the veins, which expresses at the same time the feeling of the heart and the impressions of the mind—that language was the only one we had recourse to, and without having uttered one syllable, dear reader, oh, how well we agreed!

Both overwhelmed with emotion, longing to give one another some proofs of the sincerity of our reconciliation and of the ardent fire which was consuming us, we rose without unclasping our arms, and falling (a most amorous group!) on the nearest sofa, we remained there until the heaving of a deep sigh which we would not have stopped, even if we had known that it was to be the last!

Thus was completed our happy reconciliation, and the calm infused into the soul by contentment, burst into a hearty laugh when we noticed that I had kept on my cloak and my mask. After we had enjoyed our mirth, I unmasked myself, and I asked her whether it was quite true that no one had witnessed our reconciliation.

She took up one of the candlesticks, and seizing my hand:

"Come," she said.

She led me to the other end of the room, before a large cupboard which I had already suspected of containing the secret. She opened it, and when she had moved a sliding plank I saw a door through which we entered a pretty closet furnished with everything necessary to a person wishing to pass a few hours there. Near the sofa was a sliding panel. M—— M—— removed it, and through twenty holes placed at a distance from each other I saw every part of the room in which nature and love had performed for our curious friend a play in six acts, during which I did not think he had occasion to be dissatisfied with the actors.

"Now," said M—— M——, "I am going to satisfy the curiosity which you were prudent enough not to trust to paper."

"But you cannot guess...."

"Silence, dearest! Love would not be of divine origin did he not possess the faculty of divination. He knows all, and here is the proof. Do you not wish to know whether my friend was with me during the fatal night which has cost me so many tears?"

"You have guessed rightly."

"Well, then, he was with me, and you must not be angry, for you then completed your conquest of him. He admired your character, your love, your sentiments, your honesty. He could not help expressing his astonishment at the rectitude of my instinct, or his approval of the passion I felt for you. It was he who consoled me in the morning assuring me that you would certainly come back to me as soon as you knew my real feelings, the loyalty of my intentions and my good faith."

"But you must often have fallen asleep, for unless excited by some powerful interest, it is impossible to pass eight hours in darkness and in silence."

"We were moved by the deepest interest: besides, we were in darkness only when we kept these holes open. The plank was on during our supper, and we were listening in religious silence to your slightest whisper. The interest which kept my friend awake was perhaps greater than mine. He told me that he never had had before a better opportunity of studying the human heart, and that you must have passed the most painful night. He truly pitied you. We were delighted with C—— C——, for it is indeed wonderful that a young girl of fifteen should reason as she did to justify my conduct, without any other weapons but those given her by nature and truth; she must have the soul of an angel. If you ever marry her, you will have the most heavenly wife. I shall of course feel miserable if I lose her, but your happiness will make amends for all. Do you know, dearest, that I cannot understand how you could fall in love with me after having known her, any more than I can conceive how she does not hate me ever since she has discovered that I have robbed her of your heart. My dear C—— C—— has truly something divine in her disposition. Do you know why she confided to you her barren loves with me? Because, as she told me herself, she wished to ease her conscience, thinking that she was in some measure unfaithful to you."

"Does she think herself bound to be entirely faithful to me, with the knowledge she has now of my own unfaithfulness?"

"She is particularly delicate and conscientious, and though she believes herself truly your wife, she does not think that she has any right to control your actions, but she believes herself bound to give you an account of all she does."

"Noble girl!"

The prudent wife of the door-keeper having brought the supper, we sat down to the well-supplied table. M—— M—— remarked that I had become much thinner.

"The pains of the body do not fatten a man," I said, "and the sufferings of the mind emaciate him. But we have suffered sufficiently, and we must be wise enough never to recall anything which can be painful to us."

"You are quite right, my love; the instants that man is compelled to give up to misfortune or to suffering are as many moments stolen from his life, but he doubles his existence when he has the talent of multiplying his pleasures, no matter of what nature they may be."

We amused ourselves in talking over past dangers, Pierrot's disguise, and the ball at Briati, where she had been told that another Pierrot had made his appearance.

M—— M—— wondered at the extraordinary effect of a disguise, for, said she to me:

"The Pierrot in the parlour of the convent seemed to me taller and thinner than you. If chance had not made you take the convent gondola, if you had not had the strange idea of assuming the disguise of Pierrot, I should not have known who you were, for my friends in the convent would not have been interested in you. I was delighted when I heard that you were not a patrician, as I feared, because, had you been one, I might in time have run some great danger."

I knew very well what she had to fear, but pretending complete ignorance:

"I cannot conceive," I said, "what danger you might run on account of my being a patrician."

"My darling, I cannot speak to you openly, unless you give me your word to do what I am going to ask you."

"How could I hesitate, my love, in doing anything to please you, provided my honour is not implicated? Have we not now everything in common? Speak, idol of my heart, tell me your reasons, and rely upon my love; it is the guarantee of my ready compliance in everything that can give you pleasure:"

"Very well. I want you to give a supper in your casino to me and my friend, who is dying to make your acquaintance."

"And I foresee that after supper you will leave me to go with him."

"You must feel that propriety compels me to do so."

"Your friend already knows, I suppose, who I am?"

"I thought it was right to tell him, because if I had not told him he could not have entertained the hope of supping with you, and especially at your house."

"I understand. I guess your friend is one of the foreign ambassadors."

"Precisely."

"But may I hope that he will so far honour me as to throw up his incognito?"

"That is understood. I shall introduce him to you according to accepted forms, telling his name and his political position."

"Then it is all for the best, darling. How could you suppose that I would have any difficulty in procuring you that pleasure, when on the contrary, nothing could please me more myself? Name the day, and be quite certain that I shall anxiously look for it."

"I should have been sure of your compliance, if you had not given me cause to doubt it."

"It is a home-thrust, but I deserve it."

"And I hope it will not make you angry. Now I am happy. Our friend is M. de Bernis, the French ambassador. He will come masked, and as soon as he shews his features I shall present him to you. Recollect that you must treat him as my lover, but you must not appear to know that he is aware of our intimacy."

"I understand that very well, and you shall have every reason to be pleased with my urbanity. The idea of that supper is delightful to me, and I hope that the reality will be as agreeable. You were quite right, my love, to dread my being a patrician, for in that case the State-Inquisitors, who very often think of nothing but of making a show of their zeal, would not have failed to meddle with us, and the mere idea of the possible consequences makes me shudder. I under The Leads—you dishonoured—the abbess—the convent! Good God! Yes, if you had told me what you thought, I would have given you my name, and I could have done so all the more easily that my reserve was only caused by the fear of being known, and of C—— C—— being taken to another convent by her father. But can you appoint a day for the supper? I long to have it all arranged."

"To-day is the fourth; well, then, in four days."

"That will be the eighth?"

"Exactly so. We will go to your casino after the second ballet. Give me all necessary particulars to enable us to find the house without enquiring from anyone."

I sat down and I wrote down the most exact particulars to find the casino either by land or by water. Delighted with the prospect of such a party of pleasure, I asked my mistress to go to bed, but I remarked to her that, being convalescent and having made a hearty supper, I should be very likely to pay my first homages to Morpheus. Yielding to the circumstances, she set the alarum for ten o'clock, and we went to bed in the alcove. As soon as we woke up, Love claimed our attention and he had no cause of complaint, but towards midnight we fell asleep, our lips fastened together, and we found ourselves in that position in the morning when we opened our eyes. Although there was no time to lose, we could not make up our minds to part without making one more offering to Venus.

I remained in the casino after the departure of my divinity, and slept until noon. As soon as I had dressed myself, I returned to Venice, and my first care was to give notice to my cook, so that the supper of the 8th of February should be worthy of the guests and worthy of me.

End of the Project Gutenberg EBook of To Paris And Prison: Convent Affairs by Jacques Casanova de Seingalt

*** END OF THIS PROJECT GUTENBERG EBOOK TO PARIS AND PRISON: CONVENT ***

***** This file should be named 2958.txt or 2958.zip ***** This and all associated files of various formats will be found in: http://www.gutenberg.net/2/9/5/2958/

Produced by David Widger

Updated editions will replace the previous one—the old editions will be renamed.

Creating the works from public domain print editions means that no one owns a United States copyright in these works, so the Foundation (and you!) can copy and distribute it in the United States without permission and without paying copyright royalties. Special rules, set forth in the General Terms of Use part of this license, apply to copying and distributing Project Gutenberg-tm electronic works to protect the PROJECT GUTENBERG-tm concept and trademark. Project Gutenberg is a registered trademark, and may not be used if you charge for the eBooks, unless you receive specific permission. If you do not charge anything for copies of this eBook, complying with the rules is very easy. You may use this eBook for nearly any purpose such as creation of derivative works, reports, performances and research. They may be modified and printed and given away—you may do practically ANYTHING with public domain eBooks. Redistribution is subject to the trademark license, especially commercial redistribution.

The End

www.ingramcontent.com/pod-product-compliance
Lightning Source LLC
Chambersburg PA
CBHW072316290526
45794CB00002B/683